BAGHDAD BULLETIN

Baghdad Bulletin

DAVID ENDERS

Pluto Press
LONDON

First published 2005 by Pluto Press
345 Archway Road, London N6 5AA

www.plutobooks.com

British Library Cataloguing in Publication Data
A catalogue record for this book is available from the British Library

ISBN 0 7453 2465 7

for my brother

Contents

Why are you going to China?
—One of my roommates, when I told
her I was going to study in Beirut

Preface

In February 2003 I left the University of Michigan to spend my final semester at the American University of Beirut. I went to Beirut for various reasons, including a desire to locate distant relations (my maternal grandparents are first-generation Lebanese immigrants). I also wanted to be somewhere I could go skiing. But most of all I wanted to be in a place where American students feared to tread, where they didn't even think to go. I like proving to people that their preconceptions are misconceptions. When I was an intern for the Associated Press in Detroit, I walked the entirety of Eight Mile Road, the rough-and-ready border between Detroit and the suburbs. One side of the road was thick with urban rot; the other was edged with tidy tree-lined streets and single-family homes. My mother warned that I was going to get mugged, or worse. My entire walk took place after dark, but all I found were people. They were the people who worked in the strip clubs or hit the bars after a hard day at an auto plant. They were the people who lived along the main thoroughfare. I didn't end up dead because I was a white boy walking around north Detroit. I ended up hanging out with the people I found there.

With war in Iraq almost a certainty, Beirut seemed like an especially good place to break down barriers. I found an apartment two blocks from the Mediterranean, not far from the parking lot that had once been the U.S. embassy. (The embassy was blown up twice in the 1980s before they moved it to a fortified compound in the suburbs.) Before long I was marching with Lebanese students and a handful of internationals to protest the American invasion of Iraq. We marched in solidarity with the Lebanese demonstrators, holding signs identifying ourselves as American: the Lebanese police were too afraid to turn tear gas and water cannons on internationals. We voiced our disgust. The day the bombing began in Baghdad, students blocked the doors to all the classrooms, though most of us had already decided to skip class and attend a march to the British embassy. After the march ended I stayed with the kids hurling rocks through the embassy windows, dodging tear gas, fire hoses, and rifle butts. I was amazed. Here they were, expressing the outrage so many of my peers and I feel, but in a manner we would never dare.

My friends in Beirut often asked me, "You are an American who opposes the war. But what are you really doing about it?"

"I'm writing about what I see here," I would say. "I'm telling people in America what people outside America are saying. And I'm reassuring people here that everyone in America hasn't gone nuts."

But it happened over and over again.

I was sitting in a bar in Beirut the night the war started, with Mira and Rania, two friends who always took me to task for being American. My French was less than perfect; my Arabic was nonexistent. Here I was, a kid from the Midwest in the Mideast, just hanging out. They knew how I felt toward my government, they knew that I didn't hold the same prejudices and misconceptions as many Americans, and so we usually didn't get stuck on questions of motivation, or on questions of blame. But on that night it was all too much. Rania started crying.

"Why would they do this? Why do Americans want to make war?"

Maybe it was just machismo. Maybe it was because the distance between Beirut and Baghdad is less than that between Detroit and New York. I decided to go to Baghdad. I was in the position to do it, so why not? It was considerably less of a sacrifice than many of my compatriots were being asked to make. It suddenly became entirely real to me that a large part of the story of my generation was unfolding not too far to the east. At the very least, I could bear witness.

"I'm going to Baghdad," I told Rania.

I don't remember now if those words stopped the tears or not, though that was the hoped-for result.

"Are you serious?"

I had been talking for twenty-two years. Now I had my chance. During Easter break I would go to Baghdad. I went to the embassy and applied for a visa, standing next to a long line of Lebanese men who were going to Iraq to fight. The visa never came—the Iraqi government fell first. In the meantime I kept trying to convince my Lebanese friends to make the trip with me. I would need someone who spoke Arabic. But in the end none of them would do it. That was when Ralph called.

Ralph had come to Beirut on a whim. He was twenty-four, with a master's degree in chemistry from Oxford. He had spent some time working in a lab, but his real passion seemed to be international relations. When he got tired of the lab, he managed, with a little help from connections, to land an internship of sorts at a British daily; from there he decided to go to Beirut to study Arabic. We met because we were both freelancing for the *Daily Star*, Lebanon's English-language daily. While Ralph was home on Easter break, his mum suggested he open an English-language paper in Baghdad after the war. "They're going to need one, right?" she asked him.

She later said she hadn't meant it seriously. Regardless, it stuck. Ralph only had about six months of actual experience in journalism, so he called me. I was standing in downtown Beirut, and the only thing that occurred to me was that an open-ended trip to Baghdad might cause problems for graduation and the AP job I'd lined up.

"If you can get the money, I'll do it," I said. So I stalled my plans to travel to Baghdad and waited for Ralph to come back to Beirut. A few days later we were in Amman. This was my chance.

"You oppose the war, but what are you doing about it?"

Now I really could say I was doing something.

Ralph and I had originally conceived of the *Baghdad Bulletin* as a daily newspaper before deciding that the problems of staffing, distribution, and production made insightful daily journalism in Baghdad a pointless endeavor. I envisioned (modestly, of course) a sort of *Harper's* for the Middle East, an intellectual magazine that could somehow draw together all of the issues for which Baghdad had suddenly become the nexus. The actual paper turned out to be a little more like the *Economist* in its form, but almost entirely unique in its content. An English-language magazine in a war zone. We ran for seven issues, twice monthly, printing ten thousand copies of each issue and distributing them around the country. We were getting at least as many readers on our Web site, where the paper was available for free download.

To give an idea of exactly what we were trying to accomplish, I'm reprinting a response I wrote to a reader's letter in the summer of 2003. The letter read, in part:

As I was reading the articles I began to ponder the reality of the Baghdad Bulletin. It seems bizarre in the extreme, when one thinks about it, that such a publication would be established and set up by outsiders.

My response:

First, we do not intend to present ourselves as authoritative, only honest. The target audience of the *Bulletin* is anyone in Iraq who speaks English (and there are a lot of English-speaking Iraqis), and the plan is to eventually publish two issues, one in Arabic, one in English, with the same content. It is extremely important to have English-language reporting here on the ground right now because English speakers (the

Coalition especially) are going to be making most of the decisions—
it's an unfortunate fact, but they should be making them based on
good information, and there should be a publication here to challenge
and examine those decisions (in English) as well.

The media here should not be controlled and edited by foreigners,
and much of it is not. We are one of the many new publications in
Iraq—freedom of the press has been one of the happiest by-products
of the invasion.

The intent is not to have foreign journalists writing most of the
articles, but to begin training Iraqi journalists to take over the publication, eventually writing all of the foreign staff out of the equation
and leaving the *Bulletin* here as a locally owned and operated publication. The situation is as it is at this point because, quite simply,
there are not very many well-trained journalists here. Thirty years of
oppressive rule have taken a toll. We are encouraging Iraqi involvement as much as possible and rely heavily on the advice and contri-
butions from our Iraqi staff, which do outnumber the foreign staff at
the magazine. . . .

Iraq should demand world attention, and I suspect it is unlikely
anyone locally would have set up a Web site and magazine people
would be interested in reading internationally so quickly. We are providing a much greater readership for Iraqi writers than they would
receive anywhere else. Also, by having the company incorporated in
London and initially set up by foreigners, we strongly reduce the
chances we will be harassed by Coalition forces and can call attention to the harassment of other publications. (Unfortunately, we're
still subject to the same press prevention tactics as everyone else
here.)

Hope this makes you feel a little bit better about reading us.

Acknowledgments

These people, in no particular order, helped me maintain my sanity (and safety) as I lived and wrote this book. Shukran.

Mom, Dad, Therese, Stephen, Uncle Larry, Alaa Kamel, Ralph Hassall, Mark Gordon-James, Kathleen McCaul, Catherine Arnold, Seb Walker, Kareem Omer, Rosie Garthwaite, James Brandon, Ali Hamid Manhal, Naser Thabit, Ahmed Ayad, Salam Sadeq, Samer Sadeq, Shaalan Al-Jabouri, Shadi Al-Qassim, Rory, Latifa, Babs, Lauren and the Aposhian family, Sarah Smiles, Ziad, The H-bomb, Dr. Kubba, Yousef Alaa, Rebecca Lossin, Wisam Al-Atrachji, David Martinez, Paola Gasparoli, Isam Rashid, Yunis and his family, Nay, Jerry Marogil, Jim Reische, Christian Parenti, Dahr Jamail, Salam Talib, Eman Khammas, Jo Wilding, Rana Al-Ayoubi, Mira Minkara, and Jassim Mohamed.

Special thanks to Yahya Sadowski for letting me write my term papers in Baghdad, to Fadhil for lying to the neighbors, and to Kathleen's mom.

All articles from the *Baghdad Bulletin* are printed here as they appeared in the magazine, without further editing.

Hathahee al-hurrea!

Basically, if you can carry it away or hold onto it, it's as good as yours.

—*Mark Gordon-James, on the looting by Iraqis and the Coalition Provisional Authority*

Prologue

Agence France-Presse

6.9.03

"Baghdad freesheet hits the streets"
By Steve Kirby

BAGHDAD—A country devastated by war and occupied by U.S. and British troops may seem the least promising place to open an English-language paper, but as the first edition of the *Baghdad Bulletin* hit the streets Monday its owner-editors were confident of success.

The bi-monthly news magazine is ground-breaking in every way.

It is independent, colorful and produced to Western standards in a country used to the turgid propaganda sheets of the Saddam Hussein regime.

The *Bulletin* is also distributed free to hotels, businesses, and households across the five wealthiest neighborhoods of Baghdad so that the advertisers who cover most of its costs know they are reaching their big-spending target markets.

Getting the paper off the ground in a city which still has to contend with lawlessness, frequent power cuts and a night-time curfew has been a labour of love for the American and two Britons who conceived the project.

The trio—two journalists and a financial consultant—have been taking no wages, banking on the eventual success of their innovative but high-risk brainchild to reward their efforts.

In the month or so since they arrived to set up the paper, they say they have had to contend with Kalashnikov-toting Iraqi gunmen and jumpy U.S. troops nearly shooting them up at a checkpoint.

"There was never a time when we thought we weren't going to make it work," says British journalist Ralph Hassall. "We have always worked 'round the problem or battled until we got it done."

The 10,000-copy launch edition boasts an article by Britain's special envoy for human rights, Ann Clwyd, on how the coalition intends to preserve the evidence from the dozens of mass graves being found around Iraq, and also takes a critical look at U.S. efforts to restore power and security to the capital.

Fellow Briton Mark Gordon-James stresses that the paper's editorial line is entirely independent of the U.S.-led administration. Although all three of them opposed the war, the magazine is "apolitical."

The financial mastermind of the operation, Gordon-James acknowledges that the trio have benefited from an immense amount of goodwill from Iraqis and Westerners alike who want to see their project succeed.

But on the strength of the advertising contracts he has already sealed he expects the paper to break even after just a few issues. He has even signed up a Jordanian distributor and hopes to find one for Kuwait as well.

Among the advertisers in the first edition are Emirati airconditioning manufacturer SKM, an Iraqi water filter distributor called Action Group and Baghdad's Cedar Hotel.

The paper has been operating on a shoestring budget—a British venture capitalist stumped up start-up capital of $20,000 in return for a minority stake.

"If other companies come in with more money and better resources I am not even sure that they would do better," says Hassall.

"The fact that we were on such a tight budget means that we have run an extremely tight ship."

The trio have taken on an Iraqi partner to take care of the advertising and paid-for distribution—a pioneering Western-educated commercial printer who worked as an astrophysicist until Iranian bombers destroyed the huge observatory he was working on for Saddam in the late 1980s.

"Of course in the past we never had a free press in any respect," says Dr. Aziz Sadik. "I thought about such a business before but I couldn't because I wasn't allowed to."

The trio acknowledge that finding English-language journalists has proved a problem—years of politicisation of both newspapers and education under Saddam's regime has made it extremely difficult to find people with both the writing skills and the independence of mind.

But for the next edition, they have taken on three Iraqis—one of them an English professor and another a former employee of Saddam's propaganda sheet, the *Baghdad Observer*—and they plan progressively to employ more.

"The endgame is to set up something sustainable—run, edited and managed by Iraqis but within the framework that we are operating now," says Hassall.

Amman
4.30.03

The Al-Saraya Hotel is near the Roman theater, in the oldest part of town. The "oldest part of town" is a bit of a misnomer—most of Amman, despite being built around the ruins of a Roman city, is little more than fifty years old, having sprung up with the prosperity of Jordan and the Palestinian exodus from the other side of the Jordan River. The city sprawls blandly outward from the amphitheater into the surrounding hills. There are Pizza Huts and mini-malls; the rocky desert setting makes it feel like Utah with mosques. There is a Safeway, the last place to buy a decent jar of peanut butter before leaving for Baghdad. The sales tax is 20 percent. I suppose that's why the royal family looks so happy in the larger-than-life pictures found all over the country.

The Saraya is as far away from the sprawl as one can get in Amman, situated amid the nondescript commercial buildings and gray tenements that climb the hills around the city. The hotel is a jumping-off point for freelance journalists, human shields, and other people who can't afford to stay at the Intercontinental Hotel en route to Baghdad. I certainly can't, nor can we afford a fraction of the one thousand dollars per car that the drivers are charging to take people into Baghdad. Ralph and I have spent the last two days using ATMs as often as we can. We withdraw money from our accounts 300 Jordanian dinars (about $510) at a time, then take the cash to an exchange shop so that I'll have American currency when I get to Baghdad.

Alistair, a old-money friend of Ralph's from Oxford, has agreed to pay for my fact-finding trip to Iraq, but the funds haven't come through yet, and I max out my credit card covering the deposit on the rental of a satellite phone. It doesn't really matter much. It's not as though I'll able to use it once I get to Iraq.

Ralph is afraid that the Jordanian Ministry of Information won't give us papers to cross the border into Iraq. We don't have press passes, and we're not affiliated with any actual publication. I hop on a computer and make some *Baghdad Bulletin* letterhead and e-mail it to Mark, a friend of Alistair's in London who has agreed to meet us in Baghdad in a few weeks to set up the business side of things. But right now we're not entirely sure we're going to get into the country. Mark writes a short note of endorsement from the fictitious Royal Press Association and faxes it, complete with signature, back to Amman. A day later the passes are rubber-stamped—the MOI has issued nearly four thousand of them since the invasion began. I take the passes from the woman at the MOI and triumphantly hand one to Ralph. We also have to sign a piece of paper swearing that we won't hold the Jordanian government responsible for whatever happens to us in Iraq.

Though I now have everything else I need, I still don't have a ride to Baghdad. Ralph and I had bought a car in Amman and planned to drive into Baghdad ourselves, but because we've spent a few extra days waiting for the rest of Alistair's money there's not enough time left for us both to go to Baghdad and be back in Amman to meet another potential backer, a friend of Ralph's who will be in Beirut in a few days. So we agree that I'll make the trip alone, while Ralph hangs back and tries to raise more cash.

None of the journalists seem to know any other way in, aside from the one-thousand-dollar-a-trip drivers. For most of them this seems to be their first time traveling to Iraq. Many of them ask me for advice, but I have none.

I'm wandering around near the Saraya, chain-smoking and trying to figure out what to do, when I notice a line of orange and white cars with Iraqi plates parked down the street from the hotel. Most of them are Chevys from the '80s, old Suburbans and Caprices. They're filled with packages, boxes of mail, luggage, and a variety of consumer goods. Some have satellite dishes strapped on top, these being the most popular import into Iraq since the demise of the old government. All the cars are fitted with auxiliary gas tanks for the six-hundred-kilometer trip from the Jordanian border to Baghdad. Some of these are simply jerrycans on the roof with hoses that drop down into the car's regular tank. These cars are the lifeline in and out of Iraq for anyone who is not a journalist. I approach one of the drivers and test my broken Arabic.

"Inta sifir ila Iraq?"

"Eh."

"Boukra?"

"Eh."

"Ana sifir fee sayyaree?"

"Nam."

"A-desh?"

"Hamseen dollarat."

Fifty dollars for a ride to Baghdad.

Journalists at the Intercontinental tell stories about an Associated Press television producer whose car was shot at the day before. Some of the journalists say that the only thing that saved him was reading Koranic verses forbidding stealing over a loudspeaker. Others say a U.S. convoy drove by in the opposite direction, causing the bandits to flee. All I'm sure of is that the road is potentially dangerous. But Iraqis wouldn't attack Iraqis, right? Surely these people aren't carrying much money, and surely that's what the bandits are after. I also imagine a ten-hour drive across the desert, with a group of non-English-speakers, in an overpacked car with no air conditioning.

Ralph continues his efforts to dissuade me from riding with the Iraqi convoy but gives up when I ask a single question.

"Do you have a better idea?"

I'm more afraid I'll be robbed by the people with whom I'm riding. I would probably rob a pissant kid like me. Clock him on the head with his own satphone and leave him in the desert. Why not? They can't really believe that fifty bucks is all I can afford. And of course I'll be carrying almost one thousand dollars in cash. Ralph and I figure that should last me at least a week.

I enlist Fayyez, the Saraya's manager, to persuade Ralph that riding with the Iraqi convoy isn't such a bad idea. Fluent in Arabic and English, Fayyez moonlights as a travel writer for the *Lonely Planet* guides and seems to spend most of his time inviting misfits like us into his office for coffee. He agrees to meet the two men who will take me to Baghdad and invites them in for coffee as well. After ten minutes of conversation he's satisfied that they're honest.

"When you leave, we will write down their license plate numbers," he says after they've left.

My ride settled, I go upstairs to pack. As my two A.M. departure approaches I grow nervous. I go over the trip in my mind:

Leave Amman at two A.M., reach the border at six A.M., leave the border when it opens at eight A.M., I'm in Baghdad by one P.M.

Ralph asks if I want to go out for a beer, but I demur—my stomach is in knots. I double-check my bags, test the satphone by calling my girlfriend, and finally inform my parents of my plans. I call home, and my little sister picks up. I've already told her I'm in Amman, swearing her to secrecy. Mom's not home, so I leave a message. When she finally calls back she's surprisingly calm. I suspect my sister may not have kept her vow of silence.

"I'm leaving for Iraq tonight. We're going to try and open an English-language newspaper there."

"What about class?"

"It's okay. Thanks to Lebanese pluralism, we have so many different holidays that I don't have class for another week."

"Okay, honey, just be careful."

My mother's reaction just makes me more panicky. How can she be okay with this? What if she never speaks to me again? What if this is it? By this point I'm doing enough worrying for both of us anyway. Around midnight Fayyez invites me into his office for a final cup of coffee. He does this with everyone who's leaving for Baghdad. He also invites two people who just returned from Baghdad earlier that evening. One is an American freelancer; the other works for the French nongovernmental organization Enfants du Monde.

"Before I left for Baghdad, I prepared myself for death," the NGO guy says. "I gave away all my possessions. Huh. Now I want some of them back."

I try to look cool, but I'm sure Fayyez has noticed that the cup of coffee's shaking in my hand and I can barely light the cigarettes he offers me.

I suppose a lot of people who have been in Fayyez's office for that last cup of coffee are dead now, and I suppose there are a few who decided not to go to Baghdad after all. On the wall outside Fayyez's office hangs a poster commemorating Rachel

Corrie, the twenty-three-year-old peace activist killed by an Israeli bulldozer in the Gaza Strip a few weeks earlier. She had been in Amman before her trip to Gaza and had stayed at the Saraya. So had Tom Hurndall, a twenty-one-year-old photographer who was shot by Israeli troops at a checkpoint in Rafah a few days after Corrie was killed. I'm not ready to die, that's for damn sure. I begin to wonder what the newspaper stories will say.

"He had no clue what he was doing."

"American kid killed in moronic trip to Iraq."

I can imagine Ralph trying to explain the whole thing.

"Well, it seemed like a good idea at the time."

At two A.M. I walk outside carrying a frame pack unsteadily on my back, followed by Ralph and Fayyez. The cars are loaded and parked, but neither the men who agreed to take me nor any of the other people who earlier filled the sidewalks and curbside cafés are anywhere to be seen. We wait for an hour or two. Eventually I go back inside and fall asleep.

The next day Fayyez and I go to look for the driver, but we can't determine exactly why there had been no convoy the night before.

"We just decided not to go," the driver says.

Ralph and I go to the Intercontinental to check the reports from people who are coming in from Baghdad. Is the road safe? Are there any American patrols? Meanwhile, I've met Ernie, a journalist from the *Chicago Tribune*. Ernie's a big guy, bald, in running shorts. He looks more like one of the tourists than a reporter, although seeing the motley stream of people coming and going from the press office, I'm not really sure what a reporter is supposed to look like. Some folks look like they're going on vacation. The Intercon even provides picnic lunches for the trip in. Perhaps my story about starting a newspaper in Baghdad amuses Ernie. Perhaps he just wants some company. But he offers me a spot in the Suburban that the *Trib* has hired to take him in tonight.

"It's just me and a lot of booze," he says. "Hop in."

This time I go out to the bar with Ralph before I leave, to a seedy place in one of Amman's winding souks that our friend Lee, a British freelancer, knows about. We order beers and a narguileh, and the waiter brings bread and various dips that I decide won't sit very well during a ten-hour car trip. Lee asks the waiter to provide some entertainment and begins shaking his hips and making little dancing movements. The waiter, confused at first, eventually realizes what Lee's asking for and pops in a videotape of belly dancers that looks as if it's been recorded from television. The old men sitting with us in the bar shout their approval, and we all sit and watch women from around the world gyrate in outfits that would certainly not be permitted on the streets of Amman. Cheers, boys! I may not know exactly where I'll be tomorrow, but I know I won't be here. We go back to the hotel to pick up my stuff and head for the Intercon. Fayyez, tall and lanky, hugs me and picks me up off the floor.

"Don't die. You're a good customer."

May 2003

Jordanian/Iraqi Border

5.1.03

The sun is coming up over the desert, bouncing light off the cars lined up at the border. We're near the head of the line. Our driver knew the shortcut through Jordan, and we spent last night flying through the desert on a rolling road past the American bases that King Abdullah has promised the world don't exist. Off to our right we can see the road that was used for years to smuggle oil from Iraq to Jordan. We stand outside the cars, waiting for the border to open, smoking cigarettes and drinking coffee. There are five Suburbans in our convoy. We'll travel together when we cross the border. The drivers are talking among themselves, scaring some of their passengers.

"You see this?" says Khalid, who's driving the truck Ernie and I are riding in. He points at his truck's heavy aluminum grill. "I will ram them if they try to attack us. I don't care if they have machine guns, we will not let them get in front of us."

"Machine guns?" mutters a guy from the *Wall Street Journal*.

"Sometimes they run sheep onto the road to force us to stop," Khalid says. "I will hit the sheep."

Wall Street Journal's face goes whiter.

"Hey, Dave, tell this guy why you're going to Baghdad."

I mention to *Wall Street Journal* that I'm going to open a paper in Iraq. He looks at me, confused, and I don't think it registers. He's shaking a bit and climbs back in his truck to sit down.

Khalid has three children and makes the trip three or four times a week. He'll be able to retire after a few months of this, if he wants. I figure he wants to die about as much as I do, so when we cross the border I put my feet up and talk to Ernie, occasionally offering Khalid cigarettes from the cartons I've brought with me.

Our convoy forms a V shape. The drivers leapfrog each other as they speed down the three-lane highway at 100, 110 miles per hour. It's a smooth ride, and eventually I fall asleep, waking when we stop just outside Ramadi, about 100 miles from Baghdad, in the area where most of the attacks on travelers have been taking place. The U.S. Army has been receiving reports on the attacks but refuses to patrol this area carefully; journalists even stand up at press conferences to testify about being tied up and left in the desert.

George W. Bush declared major combat operations over yesterday, when he landed an air force fighter on the deck of the U.S.S. *Lincoln,* but that means little to us. I'm not sure what to expect, and Ernie, for all his experience, admits he's not sure either. The road into Baghdad, which runs through miles of desolate moonscape, has never been entirely safe. Even when Saddam was in power, banditry was not unheard of.

Iraqi tanks litter the side of the highway. Some have been ripped apart by American fire; the back doors of others hang open as if they had been suddenly abandoned. Buses, almost completely destroyed, haloed in broken glass, were presumably used to carry volunteer foreign fighters to the front. It doesn't look like the aftermath of a battle so much as of a series of explosions that spontaneously blew out the tanks and buses from the inside. The tanks look especially incongruous in the groves near the Euphrates, where the machinery of war is dwarfed by fifty-foot date palms. Abandoned antiaircraft guns sit amid the trees or atop small hills near the highway, like museum pieces on display.

Outside Ramadi we inspect a bombed-out bridge. Ernie puts on his flak jacket. I have none.

An hour later we hit the outskirts of Baghdad, a sprawling city of mostly two-story buildings, not unlike the low-slung neighborhoods just beyond downtown Detroit. The Baghdad skyline, such as it is, is clustered along the north side of the river. Garbage is piled in the streets, some of it burning and some of it just baking in the afternoon sun, and even though Khalid has turned off the air conditioning and we're stuck in the terrible traffic, I find it hard to bring myself to roll down the windows because of the smell. I can't believe the traffic. The anarchy of "liberation" means people drive on whichever side of the road they like. Most of the traffic signals don't work, and those that do are being ignored. People are even driving on the sidewalk.

Almost all of the taller buildings, save for a few apartment buildings and hotels, served some government function and have therefore been bombed. Many are still in the process of being looted, and as we pass them we see lines of people like ants, carrying off whatever they can from the rubble. It seems strange that the bombed buildings can be almost intact. The bombs, when they hit their targets, drop almost straight down, punching holes through one floor after another. I had expected their destructive force to be directed outward, but these buildings seem to have shrunk into themselves.

We drop Ernie off at his hotel, and I help him unload his supplies—weeks' worth of water and soda and booze. I've got an empty Pizza Hut box and a few bottles of warm water. I'm still trying to figure out what Ernie thinks of the whole thing, whether he figures I'll still be around in a couple of weeks. I'm desperate for some sort of reassurance.

"Good luck," is all he says. "Give me a call sometime."

Baghdad
5.3.03

I'm met in Baghdad by Kareem, a Kurdish translator whom Ralph and I were able to find through the newspaper he works for, *Halwati*. Kareem has also worked for the *New York Times* and *Time*, and I'm embarrassed to admit that I've never met any of the well-known journalists whose names he drops so easily. Kareem is nearly thirty, a quiet, skinny guy who studied English at Salahuddin University in Sulamaniyah and once spent sixty days in a Greek prison after trying to flee Iraq. He's particularly sensitive to the Kurds' suffering under Saddam: he lost relatives in the Kurdish campaigns against the Iraqi army and the retaliatory ethnic cleansing that ensued.

Kareem meets me at the Palestine Hotel. Shooting begins in the city as night falls, but we sneak over to the café across the street, on the Tigris, where Oum Kaltoum, an Egyptian singer who died in the '70s but whose soaring love songs and improvisational style are revered across the Arab world, is blaring. A crowd of journalists, soldiers, and contractors has gathered for cold, five-dollar Turkish beers. Most of the journalists have followed the military into Baghdad from other parts of the country, and they already look like they're ready to leave. Baghdad is still a nasty place: the electricity is working intermittently, six hours a day when we're lucky, and same for the water.

Things are in such bad shape that the next day Kareem and I head up to Kurdistan with a couple of his friends and Nazar, a driver whom Kareem has hired. The plan is to find printing presses somewhere in the Kurdish north and run the magazine from there, where electrical power and other amenities will be more reliable. The drive north is a happy one. Kareem and his friends have just been to Baghdad for the first time since before 1991, when the Kurds secured de facto independence from Iraq, and with it a border running just north of Kirkuk. We drive to the strains of triumphant Kurdish music, Kareem and his pals singing along. Despite the fact the country is in a shambles, they can't hide their elation. We stop along the highway several times so that Kareem and his friends can "call Saddam," as they put it.

The road north is open, save for a pair of roadblocks set up by the Mujahedeen Khalq-e, an Iranian opposition group sheltered by Saddam, and the occasional American checkpoint. As on the road to Baghdad, we pass burned Iraqi tanks and abandoned antiaircraft artillery. They look as ancient as the pieces at the war memorial in Beirut. It seems impossible that one of these guns could take out an F-18.

Kareem tells me it's my job to do the talking at the American checkpoints, and we have no problems. Every time we pass through a checkpoint Nazar laughs, and I eventually notice that there's an AK-47 beneath a blanket under my feet in the backseat. At each checkpoint the U.S. troops search the trunk and the engine compartment.

"Why don't they ever look *inside* the car?" Nazar asks.

Sulamaniyah

5.7.03

Sulamaniyah, Kareem's hometown, is much nicer than Baghdad. Over the last twelve years the Kurds have built a mini-metropolis in the foothills of the mountains near the Iranian border. The green hills seem edenic after driving across the deserts and the plains of central Iraq, and I can walk the streets freely. I feel as though I'm in Europe, surrounded by lush parks and open plazas with monuments to Kurdish heroes. The university here is renowned for its language training, and Kareem's friends have all studied English and French and speak both easily.

We've brought Mick, an Australian correspondent for *Time*, north from Baghdad. Tomorrow he'll head for the Iranian border, reversing the route by which he entered Iraq before the war. We all go out to dinner the night before he leaves, and after a few bottles of wine and some pulls from an extra-special narguileh, Mick starts talking about his travels with the Kurdish peshmerga, who bore the brunt of the ground fighting against the Iraqi forces in the north during the invasion.

"You're smoking a dead man's hash," Mick tells me, referring to one of his peshmerga comrades who didn't make it.

Soon Kareem and his friends are singing and dancing again. The restaurant reminds me of a place in Colorado. It's partway up one of the hills overlooking the town, and the patio opens onto an impressive vista. It's a clear night, and the restaurant is full of Arabs and Kurds, one of whom Nazar manages to offend with his drunken singing.

"Take the fan belt off your head," Nazar tells him, referring to the band that keeps his kuffiyeh in place. The man stands up and shouts a Kurdish slur in Arabic, but Alan, one of Kareem's friends, defuses the situation by apologizing and singing an ode to the man, who responds with a song of his own, slightly louder, slightly more impressive in its tonal quality, a tenor wail in a language I can't understand. The two men continue to go each other one better until finally the entire restaurant erupts in applause.

Beirut
5.10.03

Ralph and I have decided that for all of Sulamaniyah's charms it's too far from Baghdad, so Kareem and I return to the capital, where we locate a printer who will work with us. He's the same one who prints *Azzaman,* the largest Arabic daily newspaper in the city. What I'm quickly finding out is that there are a number of privately owned presses, and everyone who can is exploiting them. We'll buy a generator and hope the security situation improves quickly. Many internationals balk when I tell them what I'm doing, but the Iraqis I explain it to are receptive. So we'll have to go with that. I also secure a promise of ten thousand dollars from Alistair, Ralph's old schoolmate. I imagine some kid sitting in a posh Oxford club, joking with his chums about how he owns a stake in a newspaper in Baghdad.

Finally, I make a trip back to Amman and then Beirut to pick up the rest of my stuff. I'm actually moving to Iraq. The final night in my Beirut apartment is like a funeral. All of my friends want to know about Baghdad, but no one quite knows what to say when I tell them about it. The silence is broken by my friend Jerry, who's also studying at the American University. He's from Grand Rapids, and we both went to the University of Michigan, but we never met until Beirut. Jerry's mother is Palestinian and his father is Iraqi, and now he's on the phone with his father, explaining that he's going to Baghdad with me. Jerry's father gives him an unequivocal "no," and Jerry hangs up with the matter still unresolved. An hour later his father calls back. He still doesn't want Jerry to go to Baghdad, but he has the address of an uncle who still lives there. We leave the next morning.

Baghdad
5.12.03

One of Jerry's friends from Beirut has a house in Baghdad that we can use. It's in Mansur, one of the richest areas of town, a sort of Iraqi Beverly Hills. The houses are big and gaudy, and armed guards are posted at most of the intersections. Ahmed Chalabi lives around the corner and has set up his Iraqi National Congress headquarters in Nadi Saeed, the hunt club that until recently was frequented by Baghdad glitterati, lounging with drinks in hand until the wee hours of the morning. In the 1980s it was a favorite watering hole of Saddam's, but the rumor is that he didn't go out much once the Iran-Iraq war got nasty. As if to signal the changes wrought by that war, the club sits in the shadow of Jamaah Rahman, one of the massive, unfinished mosques evidencing Saddam's tremendous lip service to religion. Nadi Saeed's main hall now serves as an ad hoc conference room where Chalabi and his staff receive dignitaries and journalists in the sweltering, fly-infested heat. The entrance into the main hall is through one of the broken windows, and the INC hasn't managed to hook up a generator. If they can't get the power on in their own headquarters, I'm not sure how they're going to run a whole country.

Mansur was the site of "surgical" bombing on the first night of the war, when the Bush administration claimed to have intelligence that Saddam was in a house in the neighborhood. Four houses were destroyed, and nearly forty people were killed. Entire extended families had taken shelter in these homes, hoping to escape areas they thought were more likely to be bombed.

"If Saddam was in any house in the neighborhood, he would have been in that one," says a woman from the neighborhood, pointing to a house teetering on the side of a massive crater. "The woman who lives there worked in one of his palaces."

"It was awful. The woman who lived in that house"—she points at part of the heap of rubble that is largely indistinguishable from the rest—"she had nine children. We found half of her daughter on our roof." The site sits unattended for months, until one day it's quietly cordoned off by soldiers. The rubble is carted out in dump trucks, and the crater is filled.

A few other sites nearby have been bombed as well, and between the dust from the rubble and the dust from the half-finished mosque, we have to mop the floor every day to prevent an inches-deep buildup of fine, whitish powder.

We have the good fortune of living directly across the street from Jalal Talabani, the leader of the Patriotic Union of Kurdistan, which means that the peshmerga on our street are on extra high alert. The looting continues all over town, but we're safe. The house that Talabani has moved into is one of the gaudiest in the neighborhood, but despite the loud decor the street is strikingly quiet. It seems that most of the people here are either lying low or have left. None of the remaining residents will tell us who the former occupants of Talabani's house were, or what happened to them. There are U.S. Special Forces in the neighborhood, as well. Sometimes we see them jogging in the morning.

The peshmerga guarding Talabani's house look shocked the first time we drive up bumping Tupac from the car stereo, but they eventually get used to us, and we even manage to hook up a line from Talabani's generator. Welcome to the neighborhood.

Baghdad
5.14.03

Our feet crunch the bits of glass, plaster, twisted metal, and other debris that litter the palace floor. The Republican Palace, a massive riverside complex off-limits to most Iraqis during Saddam's rule, is still off-limits to most Iraqis now. The CPA uses undamaged buildings in the complex as its headquarters, but if you can convince the soldiers at the main gate to let you through, you can walk around the rest of the grounds. Most of the buildings have been bombed or looted or both.

Patrick, an independent filmmaker from New York, has brought us here to hunt souvenirs. Patrick served in Vietnam at seventeen and has spent time in Bosnia and Somalia, doing aid work and filming. He's the first foreigner I've met here who hasn't been obsessed with the security situation, and even though he's obviously foreign—dressing in black from head to toe, including a watchman's cap that conceals the bull's-eye tattoo on the back of his clean-shaven head—he moves around unharassed among the street kids who pick my pockets and try to steal my satphone. He's thickly muscled, but I rarely see him eat anything more than spoonfuls of honey from a jar in his hotel room. He travels with such confidence that I even begin to wonder whether he's CIA. Maybe his apparent lack of backup is only a carefully managed deception.

Everything that was worth stealing has been taken, including light fixtures and doors. Late-afternoon light filters through a gaping hole in the center of the building, a two-thousand-pound bunker-buster atrium. Dust floats in the light, giving the whole thing a romantic, dated quality. As we gingerly descend one of the unstable staircases, we see a steel door recessed in more steel and cinderblock. There are chisel marks all over it. We wander around a little longer, but the eeriness of it all—the repetition of the grand, empty rooms stripped of almost all decoration save the molding—drives us back up and outside.

Jerry picks up some rocks from the lawn and throws them at the palace. Glass tinkles, and then it's silent again. He thinks for a moment and then climbs a tilting iron gate, uprooted by looters, trying to reach a plaque bearing the Iraqi Republican eagle that hangs above the front door. Like the gate, the sign is askew. Someone has tried to remove it, and Jerry rocks it back and forth in an effort to finish the job.

"Jesus, get down before that thing falls on you! What the hell are you going to do with it once you get it down, anyway?"

Jerry climbs down without answering.

We walk around the grounds, wary of unexploded bombs or booby traps set by fleeing Iraqi troops. An unexploded grenade round sits on the sidewalk near the pool complex, which, along with the workout rooms, has been ransacked. To our dismay the life-size poster of Saddam in a white tuxedo has been defaced. I wish I could have seen the country before the bombing and the invasion and the looting, the sheer megalomania of it all. Saddam talking on the phone outside the Ministry of Communications. Saddam in full military dress outside the Ministry of Defense. There was a picture of Saddam for every occasion; he was pasted and painted onto every edifice. In Shiite neighborhoods his likenesses have been replaced by images of religious leaders. Ayatollahs have rushed into the breach and now challenge each other instead of the former government.

"The city had a beautiful, Stalinesque quality to it," Patrick says as we make our way to the garage, which is no different from the rest of the complex. There are a number of vintage (mostly American) automobiles, which have been stripped of their wheels and engines. When Ali, one of the translators at the magazine, looks at my pictures later, he says some of the cars once belonged to political rivals whom Saddam had assassinated.

Walking out of the garage we run into a soldier, the first we've seen on the palace grounds. The place seems oddly unpatrolled, given that a large part of the CPA is housed nearby.

"What the hell are you doing in there?"

"Just looking around."

"Well hell, you're lucky we didn't shoot y'all as looters."

"There's nothing left to take."

"Well, you ought to tell us if you're going to be down there."

Baghdad

5.16.03

The first troops I speak to for any length of time are some guys from the Third Infantry Division, stationed in front of the Baghdad Convention Center. In the months ahead the defenses around the center will sprawl from a pile of sandbags manned by the often bored 3ID to a maze of fences, razor wire, tanks, and guard posts covered with the sort of netting that is supposed to deflect both the stinging sun and mortar shrapnel. Troops search everyone as they enter the intermediate zone of barbed wire and sandbags, and then again as they enter the convention center. It's standard stuff: turn, spread your legs, arms out like a scarecrow, "May I see what's in the bag, sir?"

I get so used to it that by the time I return to the States it feels strange to walk around unhindered.

The guys from Third Infantry stopped searching Jerry and me after the third or fourth time. We'd pause on the way out to share smokes and talk about the States—the 3ID had been part of the initial drive up from Kuwait, fighting their way to Baghdad. They speak openly of taking shots that tore Iraqi soldiers limb from limb. They want to talk about it, and their faces show no remorse. They tell their stories in a detached manner.

All they want to do is go back home. One guy has a scar on his scalp from a bullet barely deflected by his helmet. Another guy, Kent, from Iowa, just wants a guitar. He takes off his helmet to show me the pictures he keeps inside, including his high school graduation photo, with long hair and an electric guitar.

"See? I was badass."

Kent had a guitar in Kuwait, an old acoustic that he'd bought there but had left behind. "I'm glad I didn't try to bring my guitar up with me," he says in a Midwestern twang that, familiar as it is to my ears, seems just a little strange out here. "All the gear on the outside of our tank got shot up—my guitar would have been wrecked."

After being promised a rotation home, Kent and his buddies instead end up being sent to Faluja, one of the centers of the slowly growing resistance. "They need us to do some cleanup," he tells me the day before they move out. "They put us in all the tough spots because they know we can handle it."

I'm spoiled by this first meeting with American troops. The interactions become less pleasant over time. The 3ID guys have been in the country for some time and are used to journalists because of the embeds who rode up from Kuwait with them. But when troops from the First Armored Division begin to arrive from Germany, tightly wound and dropped into a conflict they didn't start, things will become less pleasant.

My first experience with a soldier from the First Armored forces me to miss a meeting. It's midmorning, and I show up at the gates of the Republican Palace amid Iraqis looking for jobs and answers. Some want to know where family members are; others are looking for pension checks or work: "So-and-so said they would see me, tell them Ahmed is here!"

It's three marines versus a hundred or more Iraqis, most of whom don't speak English. The marines, as often happens, have been left without a translator. I'm trying to help them explain to the crowd that there are no jobs in the palace when I'm warned by one of the marines that if I don't move to the end of the line he'll punch me in the face. I show him my press card, but he tells me to get lost. I stay where I am, daring him to hit me. He's well over six feet tall, and I'm sure one of his meaty fists would lay me out. Eventually his captain walks out to see what the trouble is, and I show my press pass and move past.

It doesn't matter much, though: I'm not on the Coalition's list of accredited journalists.

"I didn't even know there was a list."

The captain has no line of communication with the offices inside the palace. The military is responsible for securing the grounds, but not for deciding who's allowed in. I ask to have a soldier escort me to where someone who knows me can vouch for me.

"We can't spare anyone," the captain says.

"Uh, he's not doing anything right now," I say, pointing at the soldier who was just threatening me, and who has now retired inside the razor wire for a water break and some shade. We exchange nasty looks, and I watch with dismay as one of the Iraqis going to the meeting I'm supposed to be attending, the interim head of the Ministry of Electricity, walks through the gate. I recognize him, but he doesn't recognize me.

Defeated, I turn and hitch a cab to the convention center. I go through the checkpoint there and get into a Humvee with some Coalition civilian officials and a pair of officers. The vehicle takes me, unchecked, through the palace checkpoint. I've missed the meeting, but I'll be sure to be on the list the next time I show up.

Other soldiers are less combative. I run into part of a support unit at a pizzeria near my house, and after I explain to them what's on the menu and help them order lunch ("I want one of them rolled-up sandwiches and a burger!"), we sit and talk. They have more questions for me than I do for them: I've been living it, while they've been stuck in a country where they don't speak the language and it's too damn hot and they're not sure why everyone is angry.

"Why are people protesting? What don't they like? I thought they were happy because this Saddam guy was gone."

"People are angry because most of them are out of work," I

say. "The army and the Ministry of Information were both disbanded—that's nearly half a million jobs right there."

"Well, that makes sense. I'd be mad, too."

We must be quite a sight to the employees of the pizzeria, which is tricked out with cushioned booths and a big-screen TV that's usually playing Lebanese music videos: a scrawny American journalist and a gang of beefy soldiers, chowing down and discussing the mood in Baghdad. Seriously chowing down. Apparently, there's not much to be said for troop rations.

"Ask this guy if we can get some more fries. And I want a burger," says one of the soldiers, who has just finished a full plate of kebab.

The employees of the pizzeria are painfully polite to the soldiers. They've heard about other employers firing employees who were rude to the troops. If anyone tries to refuse them service, as one of the Internet cafés on the street have done (the proprietor didn't like them bringing in their guns), the Americans will demand service or even threaten the shopkeepers.

The army doesn't do much to help its troops become comfortable in their surroundings. There's no Arabic training, and soldiers must often make do without translators, even at checkpoints. I occasionally pick up one of the internal army publications, the *Liberator,* which puts out special editions for different operations. Aside from the news in Iraq, there's some minimal sports stuff off the wires and a few pages of international news, almost all of which focuses on a conflict in some other part of the world. That, particularly, seems wrong and depressing.

I've got time to talk to anyone who's crazy enough to start
a newspaper in Baghdad.

—Robert Fisk, British journalist

June 2003

Baghdad
6.6.03

The night before the first issue of the *Bulletin* is set to print,
Mark, Ralph, and I break down. The last month has been the
most absurd of my life. The day after Jerry and I came into
Baghdad, Mark and Ralph followed, driving the car that Ralph
and I had bought in Amman. Mark surprises me. He's not what
I would have expected from a patrician, London School of
Economics–educated banker. Six months before he came out
to Baghdad he had finished a six-month, mostly solo road trip
from Armenia to Iran. Now he's come out here to work for free
because he had some down time before starting a new job.
Before leaving Jordan he managed to hire Shadi, a sort of jour-
neyman rich kid whose mother is Cypriot and whose father is
Egyptian. Shadi claims to have been in the Foreign Legion, and
he seems nuts enough for this to be true. But he speaks Arabic
and has business experience on his résumé to boot. Before long
Mark hires a translator for Ralph and me as well, a young man
named Ali whom Ralph meets at one of the few open Internet
cafés in Baghdad. (In May there were so few that the café was
able to charge eight dollars an hour and still have a three-hour

line out the door.) Ali has a degree in English and agrees to quit his secretarial job at a local company to translate for us.

Soon Mark has secured a contract with the printer, hired a bunch of Ali's mates to deliver the magazine in English-speaking and high-income neighborhoods, and even found a guy to help sell ads. All this despite being stuck in four-hour traffic jams and occasionally driving over freshly killed bodies. (In Baghdad, when you see a freshly killed body in the street, you generally keep driving. Best not to ask questions.) Mark is the one who manages to jerry-rig the electrical cable we have run from Talabani's generator, splicing it into a power strip that runs our computers, the refrigerator, and a single light bulb. We put all of the above in the living room of the house, which more or less becomes our office and living quarters, the single bulb burning at all hours. The air is hotter than anything I've experienced before, and we manage to hook a couple fans into the power strip, but we have to be careful not to overload the circuit. When we talk to reporters who want to write stories about us, we try to downplay the absurdity of the situation, but they usually want to focus on it. It makes a better story, a bunch of punk kids in a war zone, idealists who are far more likely to end up in shallow graves than achieve anything.

A lot of things are tough to downplay. At one point an anti-tank mine sat on the sidewalk outside our office on Saadun Street. It's the same place Mark manages to hang a sign, a meter tall, announcing our presence. The mine, one day, simply disappears.

Ralph and I immediately set about looking for writers and reporting ourselves. The first issue, which comes out less than a month after we begin working, is written entirely by Ralph, myself, and guest writers inside and outside the country. I write my final term papers and send them back to Beirut in the week before the first issue, a pair of poli-sci analyses written mainly from research on the reconstruction of the electrical grid and a few press conferences, sleeping less than an hour a night for a week as I lay out the mag and edit stories.

Sarah Smiles, an Australian freelancer I met before leaving Beirut, contributes a pair of articles and helps with the proof-reading. We're all holed up in the living room almost all night long, chain-smoking and arguing over how things should come off. But the catalyst for discussion on the night before publication is an essay written by a British military historian. At first pass it sounds as if he's a complete racist. After mulling it over and running the piece by some of the Iraqis on our staff, we decide that the author is being a little tongue-in-cheek, adopting a neoconservative viewpoint as a provocation, explaining American and British Middle East policy in terms of the security of Israel.

But we waver. Maybe it's not a clever strategy. Maybe the author is just bigoted. At best, it's a childish way to make a point.

"We can't run this, can we?" Mark asks.

"Ali and Dr. Maan both thought it was okay."

Dr. Maan Al-Taie is head of the English department at Baghdad University and one of our writers.

"Maybe they were just saying that because they didn't want to offend us. We are their employers."

"No, I think Dr. Maan would be straight with us no matter what. He's doing this just because he wants to write."

We flip through the rest of the magazine. In addition to the Israel essay, we have an essay by Larita Smith, a seventy-nine-year-old human shield, and we're pretty sure that if her subject matter doesn't get people going (she toured bomb sites near Baghdad with her video camera during the war), her piece will at least ensure that we'll be the first publication in Iraq to print the word "fuck" in some time.

We also have an essay by Daniel Pipes, a Washington think-tank veteran and pet of conservative Israeli lobbyists. I've decided to run Pipes's essay because I want people to read the full spectrum of viewpoints, and I think his pejorative tone is quite telling. In my opinion, Pipes, who seems to actually believe in a "Pax Israelica," says what a lot of people in the

States think. Or at least he represents the line that a lot of the foreign policy decision makers are taking. His essay calls for a "strongman": a "democratically minded" Saddam to be put in charge of occupied Iraq.

It was the Pipes piece that generated the worst friction when we met with Robert Fisk a week or so ago. Fisk is a British journalist who made his name reporting on the Lebanese civil war, and one of the best-known anti-occupation journalists. I had called him in Beirut to ask his advice, and he agreed to see us when he got to Baghdad.

We met him at the Hamra Hotel, where most of the print journalists stay, although I wouldn't stay there if the rooms were free and full of cold beer and pretty girls: if anyone decides to start killing journalists, the Hamra is almost totally unguarded. It even touts its "three large parking lots" in an ad in the *Bulletin*. Fisk just shrugs when we ask him whether he's concerned about staying there. I guess he's a fatalist.

I know the meeting is going to go badly shortly after we sit down. "Oh, you're American," Fisk sniffles. He wants to know why we aren't taking an outright oppositional stance. In trying to explain his feeling that there's no point denying something that's already happened, Ralph comes off sounding very pro-Coalition. Which, I suspect, he may be, after seeing firsthand how Saddam's government worked.

Fisk puffs out his chest and prepares to preach. I shrink back, knowing what's coming. For better than half an hour he rants and rails:

"Why aren't you covering the prisoners at the airport? Why aren't you covering the fact that there is no curfew?"

"We've nearly been shot by U.S. troops after eleven o'clock. If the curfew was never officially announced, it doesn't matter—it's a practice," Ralph replies.

Fisk cuts him off and goes on for some time. We had hoped for advice, and now he's telling us we shouldn't even be bothering to do what we're doing. He's right on some counts: there are things he brings up that we should be covering; the issue is more a lack of personnel, resources, and experience. I agree with him about the important things to be covering, I agree with him that the war should never have happened.

I enlist Fisk's advice one other time, when our entire staff is at the Hamra, sometime between publishing the third and fourth issues. I ask him to come talk to everyone because the most productive thing about our first meeting was that it spurred Ralph, Mark, and me on. We were motivated as much by a desire to refute Fisk's patronizing dismissal as by anything else, and I wanted to pass the fire sparked by that ass-kicking on to everyone else. Fisk could be far harsher in dealing with staff members my own age than I could.

I see him walking by the pool and offer him a beer, and we chat for awhile by ourselves. He still doesn't mind staying at the Hamra, even though there'd be a pile of dead journalists if someone decided to lob a grenade or two over the wall onto the deck of the pool. We talk shop: what I've been covering, what he's been covering. He saw the first edition of the mag but still isn't willing to write a guest piece.

"You ran Pipes, didn't you?" he asks, eyebrow raised.

"Yeah, I did. And we've written about bad U.S. Army intelligence, prison camps, civilian deaths . . ."

He looks unimpressed as I reel off a slew of issues that he identified as most important just a couple of months ago. He then looks at the crew we've assembled and begins to ridicule each of them in turn.

"Who's the girl in the sunhat?"

"That's Kathleen."

"And where's she from?"

"Fresh out of Oxford. No journalism experience whatsoever."

"I could have guessed."

He finds Rosie too erudite, still remembers Ralph's fear of pissing off the CPA, and still doesn't like Americans. He even hushes me when I try to break into his diatribe about "what Americans really think," drawing his conclusions from a recent college lecture tour. It's the only time I try to speak, and after he cuts me off I just let him run on. I want him to piss off the entire staff.

Ben, a photographer and one of the few other journalists our age in Baghdad, begins to egg Fisk on, challenging his every statement. When Fisk gets up to leave, Ben is still on the offensive, and admits afterward he doesn't even know who Fisk is.

"What does he know? Just because he's been around longer doesn't mean shit. I bet he can't prove half the shit he talks about," Ben says after Fisk leaves. To some extent, he may be right. We find out later that the "classified files" to which Fisk claims to have access, and that supposedly detail the true number of daily attacks on U.S. troops, are almost certainly the same regular security updates that Kathleen receives via e-mail from the United Nations office in Baghdad.

But right now it's four in the morning, a few days before we're ready with the first issue, and we're not sure if we should be doing any of this. I'm worried that the neocon essay will get us labeled as cultural imperialists. I wonder if we should be here at all. We've polled as many Iraqis as we can over the past month, and virtually all of them support what we're doing, but what's going to happen when we drop ten thousand copies of this mindbomb on Baghdad? Are people going to understand what we're doing? It's four A.M.; we're stoned, out of cigarettes; Ralph is smoking butts out of the ashtray; we're alternately laughing hysterically and shouting at each other, sitting around the single light bulb in the living room, unsure of what to do. We can't believe we've pulled it off; it feels like the greatest fraternity prank of all time. A magazine in a war zone. Is this really what this place needs?

Abu Ghraib
6.14.03

I'm sitting outside the entrance to what was once one of the largest prisons in the world. It's being used as a prison camp and U.S. base now, but there are plans to return it to its full penal capacity once the mass graves have been dug up. Nothing was bombed at Abu Ghraib, which seems strange, considering that just about every other state facility in the country seems to have been hit.

I thought I might recognize the prison, but it looks unfamiliar. I was still living in Ann Arbor when Saddam released all the prisoners (the ones he didn't execute) in January, in preparation for the invasion, ostensibly hoping that they'd either join the army or create havoc once the invasion had begun. There was a picture of the exodus on the front page of the *Times*, madmen sprinting out of the prison. The government minders made sure their journalists were there to witness the event.

That picture seems wholly absurd now, as I stare up at the banality of the real thing. Abu Ghraib looks like so many of the other government buildings across the country: factories, barracks, the state dairy company, none much more than three stories high. The prison is a sprawl of walled acreage closed off by guard towers and defaced murals of Saddam: Saddam wearing a bowler hat, Saddam holding a Kalashnikov, Saddam wearing aviator sunglasses, Saddam surrounded by adoring citizens. Even the inside of the prison is full of wall-size murals.

Patrick recognizes the prison. He claims to have been arrested in Iraq before the war, picked up by the mukhabarrat and taken here, only to be driven five miles from the Jordanian border and released after the air assault began in March. He says he walked the final stretch out of Iraq.

We're on our way to Faluja but have stopped so that Patrick can try to get one of his tapes back from the army. It was taken from him near here a few days ago. He has the name of a commander with Team Silver Fox, but the longer he sits in the Humvee, the less likely it seems that he's going to get his tape. Majid, our translator and one of the stars of Patrick's film, sits in the car with me, smoking impatiently. There are people all around us waiting to talk to the officers standing at the prison gates. Like those who surround every one of the other installations cordoned off by the United States, they're looking for news of missing relatives, jobs, paychecks, information. The soldiers tell them to get lost, sometimes calmly, sometimes not. Majid gets out of the car to try and help the soldiers explain to an old woman that she has to go to the Red Cross for information about her husband, finds it hopeless, and gets back in the car to light another cigarette.

Majid impresses me, because no matter how hot it seems to get he always appears laid-back. His hair is always perfectly slicked, and his eyes are always shaded by a pair of stylish rounded sunglasses with light yellow lenses. They're the kind most Iraqis identify with American troops, except his lenses aren't mirrored.

After about half an hour Patrick returns, dejected.

"I'm not getting it back," he says.

The tape, he tells me, contains footage of the aftermath of a firefight in Faluja between Iraqis and some American troops who had occupied a police station. Patrick shot the footage a week ago, blood-spattered walls in the police station and children jumping up and down on the ruins of a Humvee. At least two Americans were killed in the attack. He was filming near Abu Ghraib later that day when he was approached by American soldiers who demanded the tape because he was filming near a military encampment.

"They told me to take the tape out of my camera. If I resisted, I might get a rifle butt in the back of the head, I might get a bullet."

He had acquiesced, hoping that he'd get the tape back later. Harassment of journalists isn't uncommon, but Patrick's independence leaves him more vulnerable than usual to arrest. But his fear soon turns to vitriol.

"At what point in basic training do you teach them to hate journalists? If you're harassing journalists, you're covering up a crime—that's been true right from the start, whether it be My

Lai or bulldozing living people. If they're coming in their helicopters and their trucks and covering it up, then they're just as
culpable as the people they're liberating us from."

Patrick is obsessed with common Iraqis, with artists and
musicians, with finding some of the beauty that still exists here
amid the chaos in the streets and the rubble of the bombed-out
buildings. That's how he found Majid, the driver and would-be
actor, who's also running a music school with his wife, despite
the hole punched through the roof of their recital and concert
hall by a bomb during the invasion.

The day before Patrick returns to the States, I follow him to
a rehearsal of the National Symphony Orchestra. A few press
people, mostly pool reporters and photographers, have arrived
ahead of us. The extra rehearsal has been scheduled especially
to accommodate a special visit by Paul Bremer, the Coalition's
proconsul in Iraq. Bremer is supposed to arrive at four thirty,
and some of the musicians glance at the clock as they rehearse
the *Firebird Suite*. The appointed time passes, but they continue
playing as Patrick floats in and out of the rows of musicians,
filming silently from waist level. The pool journalists slowly
trickle away, leaving only Patrick, oblivious to Bremer's no-
show. Patrick doesn't need Bremer; he doesn't need any of the
officials who have been planted here. More than any foreigner
I know in Iraq, he wants to cut himself off from being foreign,
not out of self-loathing or opposition to the war, but as an
understanding technique. Detachment from something means
reattachment somewhere else.

"I came in February to make a movie about a war I instinc-
tively knew was going to happen here," he says. "I wanted to get
as close to it as I possibly could be with a camera, and to be as
close to the Iraqi experience as I could be, which by definition
meant getting as far away from journalists as I could get. They
live in a rarefied world as well—a world of bulletproof GMCs
and convoys and press conferences that don't tell you anything.
The goal may be different, but they operate the same as the military. Their whole world is security."

The next day, at a press conference with Bremer, I consider asking him why he didn't show up at the rehearsal, wanting to know what could have been more important than making good on a promise to people who were already dubious of his commitment. I raise my hand.

No one calls on me, and every time I try to jump in with my question, someone else gets one in first. Maybe I should just interrupt. Maybe I shouldn't. Maybe I'll lose all credibility. Maybe they'll never call on me again. Does it matter? Do I want their credibility? Do I need it? Before I can decide, the press conference is over, and Bremer is ushered out.

The first day I met Patrick, he came with me to a press conference on one of the post-invasion military operations, large-scale raids in various parts of the country, roundups and shakedowns. He asked a long, winding question of one of the generals, making reference to the generally poor state of Baghdad in the wake of the bombing and ending with comparisons to Vietnam and one simple question:

"Are you proud of what you've done here?"

"We're only answering questions that pertain to the subject at hand."

I asked Patrick why he even bothered asking the question, knowing that he would receive a canned response.

"When they started carpet bombing North Vietnam, civilian targets, I refused to fight. They put me under house arrest, and that kind of thing still haunts me. I didn't sign up for mass murder. I couldn't believe my country would commit mass murder. . . . The only way out of this is to confront people with the truth. It's a constitutional right."

Patrick needs to get out of here. He has the thousand-yard stare. Maybe he's had it since Vietnam. I know the stare: I saw it the first night I was in Baghdad, during the shift change between the war correspondents and the postwar correspondents, or occupation correspondents, or maybe this is still a war, or maybe there was really no war at all, just an invasion with little resistance, maybe they're invasion correspondents and

I'm a post-invasion correspondent, maybe we're all just correspondents.

I hope I'll know if I get the stare. I hope if I need to leave, I will be aware that I need to leave. Catherine, an Australian journalist I met that first night, had it. She had watched a colleague die in a suicide bombing at a U.S. checkpoint. Her husband, also a journalist, was coming out to work at the end of the week, but she didn't care. She just wanted to leave. Patrick's like that now. He has been filming for more than a month, and it's good stuff. But he knows it's time to leave.

"I learned that the game is to survive these bastards. They get one hour of footage, but I still have fifty-five hours of radioactive footage. The damage that those thirty-three thousand bombs in three weeks did. No one in the States has seen the child casualties, because no one in the corporate media has the balls to show them. The problem I have with the army is one of paranoia. The problem is the army—they've committed a huge crime here, and they don't even understand it. Most of the grunts are reacting with surprise at the resentment of the Iraqis, and they can't connect the distinction to their uniforms."

Baghdad
6.18.03

My cab is stuck in traffic. I've just left the convention center and am on my way past the CPA. There are people in the street, Iraqi army officers protesting the dissolution of the military and the delays in their pay. They don't know how they will eat, and they've been stripped of the dignity of their rank. These are the same men who refused to defend Baghdad in what would have surely been a brutish and bloody street battle, who slithered away, leaving clothing and even their shoes in the street as they fled the American assault. Now they're demanding pay and reinstatement, but it is the implicit threat of an out-of-work army that scares me most. They started their protest by throwing stones at the troops who came from the palace grounds to meet them. Two of the protesters were shot and killed in the melee. Now the marchers are receding, the officers pushing their angry comrades back. Some of the advancing U.S. troops carry Iraqi officers' pistols and AK-47s (smaller than M16s and much more effective in tight situations) that they've picked up along the way.

Baghdad
6.30.03

At this point I'm mostly editing, laying out the paper, assigning stories, and running the logistics of getting reporters where they need to go. In addition to myself, we have five reporters from the U.K., all twenty-seven or younger. Ralph is working in a purely administrative position, helping with logistics and selling ads with Shadi and Dr. Aziz, our printer. Mark is still handling the business side of things and desperately trying to find an Iraqi to replace himself.

Ralph and I and our British reporters—Kathleen, Catherine, Rosie, Seb, and James—are all working for free. Everyone has paid their own way to Baghdad. The *Bulletin* is picking up their room and board. We've moved out of Mansur because the owners of the house there are planning to return to Baghdad. So now we're on the north side of town, in Zeyouna, a neighborhood full of ex–army officers and middle-class types. We rent a three-bedroom house here for $180 a month (exorbitant compared to what Iraqis would pay), which houses all eight of us, plus Shadi and Fadhil, who is taking care of the house while its owners are "on vacation." The broker offers us a six-month lease, so it doesn't seem likely that they're coming back. Fadhil agrees to stay on as a handyman and liaison to the neighborhood. It takes an extra person to make sure the generator is working, the water is turned on at the right time to fill the tanks, etc. Fadhil speaks no English, but he's learning it much faster than any of us foreign staff are learning Arabic.

In addition to Fadhil and Ali, we have nine paid Iraqi employees. Naser, Dr. Maan, Dr. Kubba, and Kareem write regularly; Salam, Ziad, Shaalan, and Feras translate and drive; and Seyamento is our cartoonist. Latifa is our cook and laundress. A pool of local freelance writers and a photographer comes and goes.

The most normal thing that happens in the course of our day is that we usually have dinner together. The rest of the time is filled by reporting, editing, and selling ads. But anything can happen at any moment. The day Kathleen and Seb arrive in the country, the neighbors shoot and kill a pair of looters on our front lawn after they try to rob a nearby house. That's about as normal a day as any.

It would probably be impossible to have a normal day with the people we've brought out. Kathleen came before she had gotten her final exam results; Catherine worked in business for awhile. Neither has any real journalism experience. Seb quit his job as the letters editor at the *Daily Standard* to come out; James had been in Yemen working at an English-language paper. Rosie, another recent grad, shipped off to Basra, to act as our correspondent there, about a week after she arrived.

The Iraqis on staff run the gamut, too: Ziad is a former accountant; Shaalan used to work with the Chinese news agency, Xinhua, in Baghdad; Salam spent sixteen years in an Iranian prison after being captured during the first year of the Iran-Iraq war. Feras was in the air force; Fadhil is one of nine kids from a family in Sadr City, Baghdad's poorest neighborhood. Dr. Kubba lived in the U.K. and has a doctorate in economics from Manchester University; Naser has a degree in political science but had been working as a baker before the invasion. Seyamento had never drawn anything for publication in his life. He's a physicist.

Their ethno/religious backgrounds are also markedly different: Salam is Christian, while Feras, Shaalan, Nasir, and Ziad are Sunni. Fadhil, Ali, and Latifa are Shiite. Kareem is Kurdish. It makes no difference. Ziad and Feras love Saddam; Shaalan keeps mum on the subject, as does Fadhil. Kareem is the only one pleased about the American presence, if guardedly so. But there are never any problems; or, if there are, they're quickly defused.

While outside one day I find Naser, Ziad, Shaalan, and Feras talking in the front yard. They fall silent as I pass, but I find out later that Ziad had been arguing about their duty as Sunnis to kill "the foreigners."

Shaalan took care of that one.

"They're too young," was all he said.

We didn't expect them to start killing journalists until October.

—A U.S. lieutenant, upon hearing that
Richard Wild had been killed

July 2003

The Guardian
7.8.03

From "Murdered at the museum"

By Libby Brooks

Sitting in the lounge of Baghdad's Palestine hotel last week, in the company of six veteran war correspondents, the 24-year-old novice reporter Richard Wild was understandably overawed. "He seemed quite quiet," recalls Jason Burke, the *Observer*'s chief reporter, and one of the group. "But we talked about how things were going, and from the small number of contacts he had he seemed to be doing well. He didn't ask me for any help, which impressed me. He wasn't in the business of free-loading."

Burke last saw the young freelance on Friday morning, when he dropped off a tape for Burke to pass on to Channel 4 on his return to the U.K. "He was very excited about a visit he'd made to a Palestinian refugee camp in the city. He'd filmed the whole thing himself, and he thought it was going to be his big break."

Wild was shot dead outside Baghdad's natural history museum on Saturday morning, as he stood on a traffic island trying to hire a taxi. His killer approached through a crowd of students, drew out a pistol and fired it into the base of his skull, before fleeing in the confusion that followed. It remains unclear whether Wild was targeted because he was a reporter, although he was not carrying his video camera at the time.

He is the 17th journalist to be killed in Iraq since the conflict began, and the first to die since U.S. forces entered the capital in April, sparking a growing wave of guerrilla resistance. On Sunday his parents Robin and Daphne spoke of their vain attempts to stop him from making the trip. "The whole family tried their utmost to stop him going. But they seem to take least notice of their parents."

His mother said that she thought the venture foolhardy. It is certainly the case that freelancers, working alone, are always at a disadvantage without the backup and staff of an international news agency. And it remains uncertain whether Wild's inexperience rendered him especially vulnerable.

Baghdad
7.5.03

The soldiers come down the stairs carrying most of Richard's belongings. Mark and I have been waiting in the front room of the house where Richard had been staying. It's nearly curfew, but after hearing that Richard had been shot, we ran into a driver I knew who agreed to bring us here.

Jason Burke, from Channel 4, has already identified the body. No one's exactly sure what happened. There are different accounts. Richard was walking alone, nothing to identify him as a journalist. Richard had been talking to American troops. He was dressed in a "military" style. He was in a crowd. He was standing by himself. He was walking. He was trying to hail a cab. What is certain is that he was shot once in the back of the head. Some people say that Iraqi witnesses ran to a nearby troop detachment, thinking that Richard was a soldier, but that Richard was only taken to the hospital ninety minutes later, by a taxi driver and some men from the street.

Mark and Richard had mutual friends in the U.K. I had only corresponded with him over e-mail. Ever since the *Bulletin* got coverage on the BBC, CNN, and NPR, we've been flooded with e-mails from people, mostly our age, who want to come to Baghdad. The messages come with resumes attached: "I'm tired of my life in corporate media. If I quit my job at CBS in New York, can I work for you? I'll pay my way to Baghdad."

Mark and I begin to fear we've created a small movement, that people don't really understand the situation out here, and that, because they're largely no different from us, they'll decide to come out. The thing is, they really aren't any different: most of them probably have as much experience as I do. We've been downplaying the risks all along. Richard came to Iraq in part because he was "inspired" by what we're doing, and he was supposed to work with us, in addition to freelancing. Maybe it was that NPR story that referred to us as "hipsters." Hipsters don't open businesses in war zones. Crazy people do. But people can identify with hipsters.

When Mark and I return to the house, it's silent. Ralph, Kathleen, James, Catherine, Seb, and Fadhil are all sitting in the living room. James is the only one not chain-smoking. Everyone's staring at the floor. We found out this afternoon that Shadi has typhoid, and, really, I'd been hoping that would be the worst news of the day. Now I'm not sure how to react. I nearly start giggling. I'm overwhelmed. I'm supposed to know what to do, but I don't have a clue.

"It could have been any one of us," Mark says. "He was one of us."

"What about the thirty Iraqis who are gunned down every day in Baghdad? What makes him so different?"

"He was young, British, a kid who was out here without any real clue about what he was doing. Just like us."

Mark is angry. I'm angry. Kathleen, I think, is trying not to cry. No one else says anything. Mark and I walk outside.

"It's just a game of numbers. It could have been any one of us."

This is the same argument that Mark and I have had a dozen

times. I agree with him to some extent: if we continue to operate in this environment, with this many people, someone's going to get hurt. He has advocated shutting down before, and now he's thinking about it seriously.

"Everyone knows the risks. Everyone knows they can leave anytime."

"But I think judgment is affected simply by being here."

"I don't think any one of us would be in that position. We don't even know why he was shot."

"It doesn't matter. We know he was singled out for being a foreigner."

"I trust the people we work with to let us know what we should and shouldn't do."

"But you do the same stuff. You don't wear a press pass on the street, you take cabs and walk around."

"So we have to be extra cautious. This doesn't represent a trend."

Mark is still worried that the news will be reported before Richard's family is told, and that the families of our staff in the U.K. will worry if they hear the news with no name attached to it. We go inside and suggest that everyone call their parents. Mark starts making a list of everyone's home phone numbers.

"You could at least wait until tomorrow to do that."

Mark doesn't answer.

Ralph suggests we all buy guns. I'm not sure if he's serious.

What we do end up doing is hiring a guard. Fifty dollars a week, and he'll work from eight in the evening until eight the next morning. He brings his own Kalashnikov. His name is John, and we hire him because he's a nephew of Salam, one of the drivers we've hired, so we figure he'll be trustworthy. We know the price is outrageous, but we figure that it will increase his incentive to be vigilant. Whatever the hell that means. I feel bad that we've hired someone in addition to Fadhil, but Ralph, Mark, and I agree that we don't want Fadhil to have to stay up all night. In fact, John's job—sitting in our driveway with an assault rifle on his lap for twelve hours—sounds miserable. I'm not really sure how his presence helps. Fadhil has already lied to the entire neighborhood, telling them that we're heavily armed and that each of us has a gun in our room. If anyone wants to hurt us, they'll probably bring a few friends along or just huck a bomb over our front gate. Surely they won't be deterred by a sleepy man with a Kalashnikov.

I offhandedly inspect the gun while I'm outside having a cigarette. It looks as though it's at least twenty years old, and I wonder if it even works. I recall a conversation with some American soldiers about the Kalashnikovs.

"Yeah, they're accurate as hell—for the first shot," one of the soldiers told me. "Then you're lucky if the thing hits anything or if it doesn't jam up."

Right now there doesn't seem to be much chance of John even getting off the first shot. He has fallen asleep. I nudge him awake, offer him a cigarette (he doesn't smoke), a cup of coffee, leftovers, a book to read, anything. The job seems awful, but he declines all of my offers.

"Tislam," he says. "I'm fine."

I give up and go to bed.

Sleeping on the roof ensures that I never sleep in. As the sun creeps over the low roof wall, it hits my face in a slow burn, impossible to sleep through. For some reason there are always flies in the morning as well, and though covering my face with my sheet staves them off, it soon becomes stifling. I wake everyone up as I make my way down to the kitchen to fix coffee.

Turkish coffee is simple. Heat water, dump in extra strong coffee, stir. It comes out looking like motor oil. My roommate in Beirut had a girlfriend, Hiba, who, after she stopped spending the night, intimated to me that the thing she missed most was my coffee in the morning. I'm wondering what happened to her as I walk out into the driveway with my cup of coffee. I find Kathleen in her pajamas, the Kalashnikov across her chest. I spin and head back toward the kitchen.

"Jeeeeeeeesus! What the hell are you doing with that?" I shout at her from inside the kitchen.

"John just gave it to me when he left. I was the only one awake. He said he couldn't walk around with it during the day."

"Makes sense. Point it at the ground, for chrissakes."

Fadhil, awake now, walks through the kitchen and straight outside. I watch as he disarms Kathleen with one swift motion and clears the gun. The clip wasn't in, but there was a round in the chamber.

John shows up faithfully every night for the next week, and every night he falls asleep. We try to wake him up by inflating plastic bags and popping them next to his head, but it doesn't seem to work. The concerns the staff has about security seem to be fading, and I convince Mark to let John go. We buy his gun for fifty dollars and give it to Fadhil. The gun soon becomes a piece of the furniture. Fadhil stays up all night with the Kalashnikov, watching music videos or soft-core porn on the satellite. In the morning I generally find the gun on the couch and Fadhil asleep on the floor nearby.

A few days later Feras is teaching Kathleen and Ralph how to use the Kalashnikov when I wake up. I sit down with a cup of coffee, and he offers the gun to me after expertly breaking it down and reassembling it. It's an amazingly simple piece of machinery, spring-loaded, with two firing settings (automatic and burst) and only three pieces: barrel, spring and firing pin, and stock. Four, if you include the clip. It's the ubiquitous weapon of the Middle East and insurgent armies around the world, easily produced and maintained.

"Do you know how to use this?" Feras asks me.

"I just aim it at whatever I want to kill and pull the trigger, right?"

Ramadi
7.13.03

Staff Sergeant Hubert Howell is part of a small force occupying a former police station in Ramadi. Howell is Jamaican, one of as many as fifteen thousand U.S. soldiers in Iraq who aren't even U.S. citizens—approximately 10 percent of the force. He and two other soldiers are posted in the station lobby, facing Ramadi's main street. They're sitting ducks, and they know it. They point out nearby buildings pockmarked with bullet holes, places where they've returned fire. They're shot at regularly, mostly potshots, spray and run, but they're not optimistic. The fire has been getting heavier. People have been using RPGs. Mortar rounds. They can't pursue their attackers. There are thousands of soldiers sitting in similar spots, guarding an endless array of newly occupied buildings.

"A lot of people might think it's calmed down, but it's just beginning," Howell says. "Evidently it's an organized force—somebody's got to be giving them those mortar rounds. . . . It's starting to get more consistent."

"Maybe it's because we're pissing people off," another soldier says. "We shot a guy the other night, but we don't know if he died or got away—just like everything here," the soldier says.

"They're probably young kids."

Tikrit
7.22.03

The tank is rolling down the street toward me. I came outside when I heard the shooting: first Kalashnikovs, a hollow popping sound, the light-arms fire of local irregulars, then the heavier return fire of American troops with their M16s, not as loud as the Kalashnikovs but steadier and faster, then the pounding of a tank gun, five shots in rapid succession that shake the windows of the Red Crescent office Feras and I have come to visit. Now the Iraqis in the office are shouting at me to get back inside the building. I step out into the street to get a better view of the soldiers coming toward me, flanking the tank. People are still yelling at me to get back inside. I slowly raise my camera, watching for any sudden movements from the troops that might signal they think I'm a combatant. I see one of them look at me, point his rifle, check me out in his scope, decide I'm not a threat, and sweep his rifle back across the street, looking for the men, boys, whoever was shooting at him before.

They're still yelling at me to get inside.

"Don't worry, I'm American!" I shout back, remembering with a start that Feras has already told them I'm Dutch.

As though my being American somehow protects me. I figure it can't protect me any more than wearing a flak jacket, which I've neglected to do. I came up here to talk to people, and I figured it would be rude to sit with them while wearing a flak jacket.

Feras likes to tell people I'm Dutch, though virtually none of the Iraqis I've spoken to seem to have a problem with my being American. In fact, some of them embrace it: an American civilian living in a Baghdad neighborhood is a bit of a cause célèbre. It gives people something to hope for. "If he's willing to live here he must think it's going to get better. And he's American. He must know what's going on."

I don't think the people at the Red Crescent office would mind my being American, but this is Saddam's hometown. His sons, Uday and Qusay, were gunned down further west yesterday by American troops, and Feras thinks anti-American sentiment is at a high here, especially now. Feras is willing to go places other translators won't, so when he insists on taking small precautions, I acquiesce.

Out in the street I don't wonder whether what I'm doing makes sense until after the tank rolls up to the corner of the building and swivels its 25-millimeter gun in my direction. I stand there staring up the barrel, five feet away from my head. I know I should be scared, but for some reason I'm not. Maybe it's because five minutes ago this street was not a combat zone, and it seems impossible that it can be now, that there can be a tank here, this is a residential street, an aid office, my tax dollars paid for that thing you're pointing at me, for chrissakes—what the fuck do you think you're doing?

Go home! They've lied to you. There are no weapons here!

Saddam didn't even give his army orders to fight. I work with a guy who tells me that every day, who's angry at Saddam, his beloved leader, for not giving his army the orders to fight. Don't you understand? This is all a terrible mistake, and there are lots of people who don't want you here, and they'll never stop fighting. Don't you get that? This street, right here, this street is endless.

The gun stays trained on me for ten seconds, maybe less, before the turret swings away. One of the students in the Red Crescent doorway reaches out and drags me back inside. I decide to climb onto the roof instead. It's probably a better vantage point anyway.

On the roof I move slowly and wait until I've been seen by one of the soldiers before I begin taking pictures. Other than tracking me with their gun sights, they don't acknowledge me.

Maybe they do know I'm American. It was a big thing in Beirut, as well, to be an "American" American. There are lots of Lebanese kids with dual citizenship, but few who are just there. You become a guest in homes; you're suddenly popular for something you hate admitting to. Being American means being prosperous, it means you have a chance, it means you can make an unlimited amount of money. There's more resentment toward Americans in Lebanon than in Iraq, because Iraqis have had someone else to vilify for so long. But now that Saddam's gone, we'll have to see whom they choose instead.

After the troops move past the Red Crescent office and turn down another street, we go back to our lunch of homemade bread, fried eggplant, and tomatoes. The students want to know what I think about Saddam, the lies the world has told about him.

"You can't prove all that stuff about mass graves. No one really knows who did that," one girl says.

I look to Feras for help, but it doesn't matter. She speaks English—he can't make what I say acceptable when he translates it.

"No, I suppose you can't."

Sometimes I argue. When discussions turn to the "Zionist plot" or the "the Mossad was behind the September 11 attacks" theory, I try to explain why that's unlikely. But a lot of conversations still end when we begin talking about what for many here are inalienable truths: that the invasion of Iraq is part of a larger design, that it's a pit stop on the road to world domination.

Too many Westerners generalize about Arabs' love of conspiracy theories. There are a lot of logical reasons why people buy these stories. Living in a country with a heavy-handed secret police, where protecting yourself and your family means providing information about others, breeds paranoia. And real things happen just often enough, like the revelation that the wife of a U.S. ambassador is a CIA agent, to justify people's belief in nonsense. Given the available evidence, these theories seem to make sense. What's the difference between September 11 and the Israelis blowing up an Iraqi nuclear power plant? Innocent people die either way. It's a strike on the wrong side of someone else's border, a provocation. Blowing up a nuclear power plant in someone else's country is ruthless. September 11 was ruthless. Not allowing the Red Crescent or the Red Cross access to military prisons in Tikrit is ruthless. Not notifying families of where their detained relatives are being held is ruthless.

Baghdad
7.25.03

Mark likes to come with me when I go on CNN or the BBC because they have cold cereal in the staff kitchens. Today I will be beamed into millions of American homes at seven A.M., scruffy and dirty, live from Baghdad. I speak to people who are getting ready for school or work while Mark eats cereal.

We've been at the center of a small media circus since an article about us ran in the *Detroit Free Press*. Suddenly we're popular, but it seems wrong. There's so much going on here, why are *we* the story? The CNN anchors ask standard questions:

what is the mood there, how do your parents feel about this, what is the biggest challenge of working in Iraq? It's impossible to make it come out sounding right. I want to deviate from the standard questions, to explain:

"Well, I woke in the middle of the night last night because there was gunfire over the house. I think about ten feet over the house, but it's hard to tell just from the tracers. So I lay there for a minute—I sleep on the roof, by the way. It's too hot to sleep inside if the air conditioning isn't working, which it doesn't when the main power is off, as it frequently is. So I lay there for a minute on the roof, looking up at the tracers—have you ever seen tracers? They look like the lasers in *Star Wars*. These were red tracers. The Americans use green tracers, so the red ones meant there was just a random gun battle going on in my neighborhood, next to my house, probably gang stuff, nothing too uncommon . . . so I watched the tracers for a few minutes, or it might have been a few seconds, to be honest the gunfire isn't usually right over the house like that and I'm not terribly used to assault weapons . . . so after a few minutes, seconds, whatever, I rolled over and crawled across the roof to the door . . . I finished editing all of the stories for the latest edition of the *Bulletin* from under my desk because of the gunfire in the street . . . and, oh yeah, the man who owns the liquor store at the end of our street got shot the other day . . . He'll live, but now we have to buy our beer from the 'water store,' where our friend Ziad, the local shopkeeper, keeps it stashed in an unmarked fridge in the back."

That's the mood here. But I mostly talk about Iraqis who are out of work and the problems getting the electricity back on. Excerpt from a transcript of *American Morning*, CNN, 7.17.03:

> *Soledad O'Brien:* David, do you ever have a sense of the bigger picture outside of sort of putting the magazine out day to day? Do you ever feel like you're contributing in a bigger sense to bringing English-language journalism and journalism and the free press to Iraq?

Enders: A little bit. You do kind of work yourself into a bubble here. But we've finally got more regular e-mail contact, and we're getting a lot of support from people who are seeing our Web site and seeing some of the stories that have been being done about us, saying that this is a historic thing and that this is extremely important for kind of closing the gap between the two sort of worlds.

Everyone here is making history, lady. We're trying to make sure that history isn't written over. People in the States send us letters condemning Iraqis for being a dirty and ungrateful people: anyone who would loot and destroy their own cities must be degenerate. They don't know that the looting was encouraged by American troops, that most of the damage to Baghdad's infrastructure isn't from the bombing, bad as that was. It's from looting that the American troops refused to stop, even though Iraqis urged them to.

I often want to deviate from the questions, to grab the mic and start talking, shouting, this is madness, I don't want to be a part of history, I want to stop the history that's being written. I don't want to talk about the magazine, I want to talk about what's going on. Excerpt from a transcript of *On the Media,* WNYC radio, 8.1.03:

Bob Garfield: You have just left college; most of your colleagues have just left college or were still in college in England. There's very little journalistic experience among you. Do you have any idea what you're doing?

Enders: Well, you know, I'm winging a lot of it. I'll admit that. I did work for the Associated Press and the *New York Times* in the States, and I was an editor at my college paper, at the *Michigan Daily,* which has a circulation of eighteen thousand and publishes five times a week. So I do know how to kind of run a newsroom and, and get people where they're going. It's just like running a newspaper anywhere else. The usual suspects are a little different. Instead of the police chief, we have generals.

Of course I have no idea what I'm doing! Do you think anyone here has any idea what they're doing? I'm in over my head, the army is in over its head . . . Maybe someone has some idea what's going on; maybe Paul Wolfowitz knows the plan—to let them kill a few Americans a day for a few years, to not let the Iraqis enjoy themselves too much. A month ago no one was willing to accept the American appointment of an Iraqi governing council, but if we let the situation spiral further out of control, people might accept it as the best alternative . . . Maybe that's the plan . . . Promise them freedom, promise them prosperity, say we're doing better than the last guy. Never mind that the last guy was a psychopath.

I don't go to the press conferences anymore, Bob—all they do is lie; the men relaying the official story aren't allowed out in the street without an armed guard, and the ordinary Iraqi doesn't want to risk getting shot just to lodge his complaint in the suggestion box.

No one here knows what they're doing . . . except the zealots, the ones who don't mind losing their heads.

August 2003

Baghdad Bulletin
8.17.03

"U.N. in Iraq: Under threat"
By Catherine Arnold

Despite reassuring platitudes delivered with the studied certainty of the professional spin doctor, nobody believes the Coalition Provisional Authority's claims that the security situation is getting better; least of all the U.N.

U.N. security in Iraq now sits at Phase Four, with the largest security presence of any U.N. branch in the world. There is only one stage higher, Phase Five, requiring summary evacuation of all personnel. The security threat has been deemed so great that if protocol were strictly adhered to there would currently be no U.N. programs running in Iraq at all—Phase Four demands the cessation of all programs in a country until security improves.

But despite concerns from U.N. security specialists and field workers—agreed that the situation is in fact worsening, particularly in the light of the recent bomb attack on the Jordanian embassy and the tragic deaths of two aid workers—the U.N. is coming under immense pressure from the United States to downgrade the threat.

A U.N. source who spoke on the condition of anonymity predicted the security alert will probably be downgraded to Phase Three before the end of August, irrespective of augmented security fears. Meetings are already believed to have taken place between U.S. officials and top U.N. representatives to broker a deal—greater involvement for the U.N. in return for downgraded security.

Four months after the invasion, an anxious CPA is eager to send home the message that if nothing else, their troops are bringing the security situation under control. A U.N. endorsement of this would buy greater international credence than any number of earnest proclamations by CPA spokesmen.

Despite official impartiality, the U.N. has had to tread a political tightrope since the invasion simply to maintain a presence here at all.

"The U.S. hugely underestimated her involvement when she rushed into the recent conflict," said another U.N. employee, also speaking on the condition of anonymity. "They were not welcomed with open arms, they did not anticipate nor can they deal with the strategic ace that Saddam dealt when he released dangerous criminals into a city without a police force, nor did they adequately anticipate the law and order problems stemming from social unrest and infrastructure problems. The last successful intervention of this type was in Kosovo where a U.N.-led attack was immediately followed by a U.N. civil administration and police force to fill the law and order vacuum. Even Bremer has admitted that Baghdad will attract all the weirdos of the world."

If specifically anti-western terrorist organizations gain a foothold, there could be serious consequences for the U.N. Groups with political or social agendas will usually avoid targeting aid organizations, but they provide soft targets for fundamentalist groups bent on flushing out any western presence.

The U.N. is already preoccupied with the potential threat from disillusioned parties in Iraq who have failed to make the distinction between U.N. as aid agency and the U.N. Security Council that brought sanctions to Iraq. The widespread availability of rocket-propelled grenades further adds to the U.N.'s security nightmare.

At the weekly NGO security meeting, a rapt audience of nervous-looking aid-workers listens as Jean-Luc Massard, head of U.N. security, enumerates the latest hot-spots and the week's security issues. Ending the official brief the discussion is opened to the floor and hands fly up, each eager to alert the community to individual security threats encountered. It bears more than a passing resemblance to a group therapy session—except that no one expects a resolution to the problem.

Baghdad

8.20.03

The Canal Hotel, the building the U.N. uses as its local headquarters, has just blown up. One corner of the three-story building has collapsed, burying twenty-two people. I felt the explosion in our apartment, a quarter mile from the site. My ears popped, and then I heard the tinkling of our neighbors' windows shattering.

Rosie's shouting; she and I hop into the car with Salam and are there in less than five minutes, before the military arrives. I walk toward the building, past the flaming cars, and am soon the only journalist in the cordoned-off area. My first thought is to try and help dig people out. I curse myself for having never taken a first aid class. Some of the dazed U.N. staffers are talking to people buried in the rubble, but the pieces of concrete are too large to move. A bulldozer arrives with surprising speed. I walk across the front of the compound to where medics are setting up a field hospital. People are being brought out on stretchers. Salam has already taken some of the first people out of the building to the nearest hospital. Later we'll watch footage of him taking away the wounded on Al-Arabiya; his picture will be on the front page of a couple of the Arabic papers tomorrow.

I shoot a roll of film but am relieved when a pair of soldiers shove me back outside the cordon. The BBC is calling, and I go on the air almost immediately, as the first military copters are arriving to take away the injured. After I get off the phone I find Catherine, who arrived shortly after we did. We walk home against traffic, past correspondents still rushing to the scene. There's the BBC reporter, finally arrived. She's wearing a flak jacket for some reason.

Later we'll discuss whether the bombing has signaled the end of the *Bulletin,* whether it will be impossible to survive as an international presence after that day. The bombing has brought out the differences in our thinking. I had fully expected the U.N. to be attacked. Kathleen had not.

The U.N. spokeswoman who went on the BBC just before me purported to be shocked and mystified by the bombing. I'm frustrated that already things are being distorted, that tonight on television it will look like another effect without a cause. For more than a decade many Iraqis have blamed the U.N., as much as the U.S. and Saddam Hussein, for the state of their country. The U.N. had been attacked twice in Baghdad since 1998. I feel compelled to report what has happened as much to justify our own presence here as for its "news value."

Kathleen is still shocked by the deaths of "innocent people," people who were just "here to try and help." She doesn't understand how I can accept what happened as a matter of course. I try to explain that the U.N., for better or worse, is widely seen as an accomplice to the occupation. She won't buy it, and before long we're not even arguing the same point. She's just appalled at such death, up close. Occasionally I think of the bodies being carried out of the building, and each time I do, I move my mind to something else as quickly as possible. Seb had almost gone to a press conference at the U.N. building when the bomb went off but had opted out because he didn't think he'd make it through crosstown traffic in time.

Fisk's *Pity the Nation* is sitting on a table nearby, and I walk over and thumb through it, ignoring Kathleen for a moment.

By chance, I land on the pages that describe the atrocities at Sabra and Shatila in 1982. I hand it to her.

"Read this."

It's not particularly relevant to the situation in any way, except that it describes another atrocity. The deaths of innocents deemed necessary by another faction. I leave the room and come back with a glass of water for Kathleen, who's sobbing uncontrollably by now. I start to feel a bit bad for handing her the book.

Mark and I note a general curve among our incoming journalists. They all go through shock at first, some worse than others. This is followed by a wave of desperate optimism, a great need to believe that things will get better. It's as much as anything an *unwillingness* to accept that the situation could really be as bad as it appears, complicated by a growing sense of detachment. In a city this large and sprawling, something that happens on the other side of town can sometimes seem like it never happened at all.

Eventually, though, a frantic despair sets in, a sense of the infinite gulf between what is said on the streets and what we hear at the press conferences, a chilling realization that the people in charge are locked inside a security bubble, afraid to walk the streets of the country they're supposed to be helping. Watching as people are killed, as human beings mete out unthinkable violence. Sobbing in the houses of victims, knowing that the number of people who have died will always remain an estimate, the heaping of misery upon misery.

Somehow this country is to be democratically run by a generation raised through a revolution, a war, a police state, another war, an invasion, and now this occupation—a generation that has seen nothing but brutality and bombing. A generation that cannot afford to trust its elders. The newcomers' optimism is replaced by despair because the reconstruction is much more than physical, and it is not subject to deadlines, and there is no formula for success, and the formula that is being applied, such as it is, seems to be going terribly wrong.

Basra
8.22.03

Everyone knows I need a vacation. The bombing seems to be a good enough justification, but I'm not really sure Basra is the best place for a break. Rumor is that the temperature here tops 70 degrees Celsius, but no one seems to have a thermometer. They don't go out during the day, and when I make the mistake of running outside barefoot to answer the satphone one afternoon, I have to doubletime it back into the house to save my feet from the burning tile. The heat melts doorknobs.

Since I can't afford the "American price" at any of the hotels, I'm staying with a family that Rosie and Seb met on the train from Baghdad a few weeks ago. Ehmad, the head of the family, and his wife have four kids. I sleep outside while they share a single bed inside, directly under the air cooler.

I'm not quite sure how to explain air coolers, but they work about as well as air conditioners and cost a lot less. A big circular fan blows air over chilled water. They're so loud you have to shout over them to be heard. But it beats baking in the heat. They're ubiquitous in Iraqi homes.

The house is actually the guard's quarters on the grounds of a larger home vacated by one of Saddam's mukhabarrat during the invasion. Ehmad and his family are recent arrivals. Ehmad's friend Bassem had formerly occupied the single room with his wife, but they've now moved into the big house.

The British soldiers who control Basra are a nice change of pace. They've pretty much pulled out of the city, rather than tooling around the streets with tanks, American-style. Ehmad's brother was killed at a checkpoint in Baghdad recently, after missing the cue to stop, but while there have been scores of such stories from the capital, I haven't yet heard any from Basra.

The city is quite a bit more laid-back than Baghdad. Things have been quiet here since the unemployment riots a few weeks ago. The posters of Saddam have all been replaced by posters of ayatollahs, and it all reminds me of a friendlier southern Lebanon. It seems as though every other person I meet here has been in prison at one time or another. Most of them speak of karhaba (electricity) and point at their groin when they talk about their experience.

Though the British troops are less of a presence on the streets, they're just as freaked out as the Americans. And for good reason. As we're driving through town we stumble into the aftermath of an ambush: a British patrol had just left their base, the former mukhabarrat headquarters in the center of the city, when a car pulled in front of their SUV and braked hard, forcing it to stop. Another car came up behind the soldiers and opened fire. Three of the troops were dead before the other two could get out of the car. The soldiers at the scene scream at me for taking pictures and kick the bike tire of a kid who gets too close.

The most serious problem in Basra seems to be the strength of the fundamentalist factions. Fawzia, Bassem's wife, used to be a drama teacher, but even though some schools are back in session, hers is not. Theatrical and musical performances have been indefinitely canceled by order of the Islamic militias, and the local musicians have to practice on the sly.

The fundamentalists are going to have to do a much better job if they want to stop the corrupting influence of Western culture, though. Even though Ehmad supports his family of six on the thirty dollars a month that he earns from the grocery store he co-owns, he, like most other locals, has still found the money to buy a television and DVD player.

I've got a copy of *Three Kings*, Spike Jonze's mid-1990s heist flick–cum–Gulf War parable that I purchased on the streets of Baghdad, complete with Arabic subtitles and all of the sex (but not the violence) edited out. I'm amazed by Ehmad's reaction. He knows that the account of U.S. soldiers aiding the Shia intifada after the 1991 war is false. He knows what really happened, and he knows that soldiers don't look like Marky Mark, Ice Cube, or George Clooney; but he wants to believe it.

"This is a wonderful film," says Ehmad. "It paints the Shia as heroes. And the Americans help them." And I'd been worried that he'd be mad at me for letting his kids watch such a violent flick.

The love of American popular culture here blows my mind. The one thing that horrifies me almost as much as the reports of American troops committing cold-blooded murder on a daily basis is the success of violent action movies. Despite the censorship, Shabab TV often showed bootlegged American films even during Saddam's time. This explains why so many Iraqis, having never left the country, speak English with an American accent. It also explains a few other things, like why so many Iraqis were initially sold on the idea of an American invasion.

I'm often asked questions like the following:

"In the movies Americans are all rich and drive nice cars. They respect the rights of animals. And all Americans are beautiful. What happened to the troops? Most of them are ugly."

"You shouldn't believe everything you see in American films," I say. "That's not really what the country is like."

"But Ronald Reagan, an actor, became your president."

The need to believe in the American myth, as portrayed by the movies, seems to run deep here.

"I cried when I saw *American Beauty*," one man I know tells me while I am interviewing him about his brothers, who have been arrested by the U.S. military. "I cried when I watched *Titanic*, too. We love American culture, but we support what the resistance is doing."

Shabab TV also showed reruns of *Friends*, the underlying message of which is: despite the fact that you may not have a job, you can live in a big apartment in New York with a nice view.

The video stores offer bootleg DVDs for less than a dollar each, complete with people standing up in front of the screen and clapping at the end. Kevin Costner is still a big deal here.

Abbas, one of the guys about my age who lives in my neighborhood, doesn't speak much English, but he loves action movies. He can reel off the names of hundreds of actors and titles, each with a big smile and thumbs-up.

"CLINT EASTWOOD GOOD!

"VAN DAMME GOOD!

"*TERMINATOR* GOOD! *TERMINATOR 1* AND *2*, GOOD! NOT *TERMINATOR 3*!"

Special effects seem to have led to some misunderstandings. In a country without cell phones, movies have created the illusion that Americans possess the technology to do just about anything. It's the ground-level stuff we're not good at. There's a widespread belief that the mirrored shades worn by American soldiers are endowed with X-ray vision. So why can't the most powerful country in the world get the power back on?

On a ride-along with the Iraqi police, one of the officers posed what I thought was a strange question.

"Do you like pornography?"

"Uh . . . not particularly."

"I thought all Americans loved pornography."

"No."

"But aren't most porno movies made in America?"

"That might be true, but that doesn't mean everyone watches them."

To be fair, I thought it was the Iraqis who were obsessed with porn. Their ubiquitous satellite dishes largely decode adult stations and a few news channels. In fact, were it not for the pacifying effect of all that televised flesh during the hot summer, popular armed resistance might have begun much sooner.

Iraqis aren't the only people here who are a little confused about American values. At a women's prison in Baghdad, a military policeman, a former truck driver from Ohio, tells me that one of their biggest problems is women trading their prisoner identification bracelets, either to get more medication or simply to mess with the guards.

"I wish we could just tattoo numbers on them when they came into the prison," the MP says. "That would make it so much easier. Just like that science fiction movie where they did that. What was that movie? It was a really good one, that science fiction movie where they tattooed the numbers on the prisoners."

Another MP, seated on the other side of the room, pipes up. "You mean *Schindler's List?*"

Umm Qasr
8.23.03

I've made the hour-long trip from Basra to interview John Walsh. Walsh is head of SSA Marine, the Seattle-based company in charge of getting Iraq's main port back in working order. It seems like a good way to start working on a story about the corporatization of Iraq. Somehow, though, the reconstruction doesn't seem to be working out the way a lot of people thought it would. Walsh ultimately declines the interview: he has been receiving death threats and is being blamed for fuel shortages in Basra, and so apparently isn't eager to bring further attention to himself.

The frustrating thing is that while foreign companies aren't moving in here as quickly as was expected, little is being done to improve the local infrastructure, either. Most of the goods coming into the port are food aid, handled by the World Food Program. People in Basra are forced to get clean water from UNICEF tankers. The few companies that are here are mostly keeping a low profile and doing little to help anyone, even— surprisingly—themselves. If the reconstruction money is being spent, it's hard to figure out where. The best guess is that firms are spending it on security or stealing it outright. Attacks on foreign companies are steadily on the increase, and the Green Zone is locked down more and more often. The guerrillas know who they want to hit. Reconstruction is a myth.

Basra
8.24.03

Rosie's taking the chance to get a little R&R while I'm down here, so I'm working with her translator, Mo. We're on our way to the desert outside Basra to look for people living near Iraqi tanks destroyed by the United States in the second Gulf War. (Iraqis refer to the Iran-Iraq war as the first Gulf War; the 1991 conflict that Americans think of by that name was the second Gulf War here.) The cancer rates in these areas are abnormally high. At Tamimi Hospital, the main hospital in Basra, one of the doctors has done long-term studies of people living near sites hit by rockets and other depleted-uranium munitions in 1991. He's finding patients with three different types of acute cancers at the same time, types that can only be explained by exposure to radiation. One of his study groups is made up of the doctors at the hospital itself, who also evidence abnormally high cancer rates. Many of them have died or are dying. The hospital was bombed in 1991.

Basra fared much worse than Baghdad in the first war with the United States. The bombing was heavier here, and so was the fighting. The signs of battle are still everywhere: buildings sitting across a field from each other are riddled with holes inflicted by the artillery of opposing armies. There are tank graveyards, too. Many weapons lie where they were discarded or destroyed, and that's what Mo and I are looking for.

Mo himself is a great find. I'm amazed he's still in the country. He worked for the British Army before the invasion, calling in target coordinates on a smuggled satphone. His mother is British, and he grew up in London, moving to Iraq to live with his father when he was fifteen. His mother wants him back, but Mo wants to stay here and see the country rebuilt.

Mo is generally fearless, so I'm a bit worried when he wavers about visiting the outskirts of town. Eventually he agrees to go: I guess he figures I'm going to go either way (he's right), so he might as well be there to bail me out. The small hovels and junkyards outside Basra look like a *Star Wars* set: I'm waiting for a bunch of mookish little guys to attack us with sticks, but instead we find two guys pushing handcarts loaded with rolls of heavy power cable along the side of the highway. The police pass as we stand there, and the British army is about five minutes behind us up the road, but these guys clearly don't care.

A lot of people believe that the organized crime rackets control Basra, and looting copper wire is supposedly one of their biggest businesses. The wire is melted down and the copper sold to Iran and other neighboring countries. This is a clear indication that the CPA's "job creation program" (paying seventy thousand or so people two dollars a day to pick up trash and clean out irrigation ditches) is not working as planned. Many Iraqis suspect that unemployment is what really fuels the resistance.

I get out of the car and start snapping pictures of the looters from the other side of the road. A couple of guys quickly roll up behind us in a brand-new white Caprice (a lot of people in Basra have nice new cars: a BMW two-seater, the kind James Bond drives, can be picked up for about three thousand dollars) and politely ask Mo what the hell I think I'm doing.

"He's trying to show the plight of the Iraqi people."

Good. Very diplomatic.

"Is he a foreigner?" one of the guys asks Mo. "Hooee aj-nabi?"

"Yes."

"Is he with you?"

"Yes."

"That's lucky. Otherwise we would kidnap him right now."

Ehmad insists on holding my hand whenever we go anywhere in town. I've been trying to explain to him that American guys don't usually hold hands. But suddenly I find it very reassuring that he's willing to do it.

Baghdad

8.30.03

We make a concerted effort to ensure that the *Bulletin* gives a wider view of the situation in Iraq than most media outlets—to show that the vast majority of people in this city of six million are not directly involved in the fighting, though of course everyone has been affected by the violence in one way or another. People are desperately trying to restore some sort of normality to their lives, but it's not easy. Unemployment is, at best guess, around 70 percent, and strong family structure is about the only thing keeping many of the jobless from ending up on the streets. Inflation is skyrocketing, and squatters are filling the bombed and looted ministries. They're occasionally shooed out by the army patrols who have finally gotten around to clearing unexploded ordnance, but in the meantime these buildings have become teeming tenements. In Basra the British troops always say they're removing U.S. ordnance; in Baghdad the U.S. troops always say the unexploded bombs are British. It doesn't much matter, though.

Baghdad Bulletin

8.31.03

"Tour de Baghdad"
By Seb Walker

One of the more bizarre sights to be seen on Baghdad's streets is men in Day-Glo Lycra pounding along the highway on racing cycles in the mid-morning sun. With the searing heat, the heavily potholed city roads, and the complete absence of road law, one might be forgiven for thinking these guys had spent slightly too long in the sun.

But it turns out that cycling is an unexpectedly popular sport, which the Ministry of Youth and Sport has on its list for regeneration.

"We have many cyclists here," said Abdul Razzaq, Deputy Minister of Sport. "Until now, the curve has been down—there were no official cycling associations. But new equipment is planned and we hope to establish a special area in Baghdad for cycling by 2004 with indoor and outdoor facilities."

But how much talent is really out there? It must be quite an amateur set-up, given all the obstacles one would have to face as an aspiring Lance Armstrong in Iraq. The minister agreed to arrange a showdown, and this hapless reporter was given the task of putting the riders at one of the top clubs in the country through their paces.

The race didn't start too well—lining up at the starting block in jeans and leather shoes, I was confronted by the entire team of Al-Sinaa Club in full battle-dress. They certainly looked the part, although coach Dhiya Al-Din Abbas claims the team has been handicapped since their locker room was looted just after the war.

"Everything got stolen by the looters, including spare parts for the bikes," said Abbas. "We used to have 40 of these Bianchi (Italian-made) cycles which are worth about $1600 each. We found many of them on sale again at the local black market for $50. They raised the price to $300 when they found out that the bikes had been used by members of the national team, saying 'This is our share of the oil!'"

After some deliberation, it was decided that just one circuit of the Martyr's Monument would be enough. I feigned disappointment, but stressed that I wouldn't want to tinker with their training schedules. So the pack moved off toward the three-lane motorway which serves as the club's practice area, this writer wobbling along at the rear.

Negotiating Baghdad traffic in a vehicle made from reinforced steel is a frightening enough experience—on a bicycle, you are truly at the mercy of the unpredictable taxis and battered lorries thundering along the tarmac. As I struggled to keep pace, it quickly ceased to be a matter of who would come first and instead became one of self-survival.

In the event, I was flanked almost the whole way on either side by the top two riders at the club, Aziz Abdul Kerim and Yasir Dhiya Al-Din. Kerim, 21, competes for the national team and won the silver medal at the national championships in 2002. His ambition is to take part in the Tour de France, but he's not optimistic of his chances.

"Cycling is my favorite sport and I would like to make a career out of it," he said. "But this will only happen if I manage to leave Iraq."

The financial rewards of success here are not enough to sustain a living—you get about $25 for doing well in the national championships.

Al-Din has been a cyclist for 13 years, which might have something to do with the fact that his father is the club coach. He is also convinced he needs to leave Iraq to find a better cycling environment.

"You get used to the heat," he said. "But I've never raced indoors—and the roads here are not safe."

I empathized heartily as I bounced into another pothole, desperately trying to keep balance as a six-vehicle U.S. military convoy roared past, the soldiers whooping at the sight of men in tight shorts.

When the finish line came into view, I toyed with the idea of making a surprise breakaway for a sprint finish. But looking around at the barely perspiring professionals with legs carved from wood who had accompanied me at snail's pace around the course, I thought better of it. Next time, I threatened, I'll bring a pair of shorts with me—then you'll see something.

"Great," said coach Abbas with a smile. "We're here everyday at 8 A.M. for three hours of training. You're very welcome."

September 2003

Najaf
9.2.03

The people who have walked for three days from Baghdad to Najaf for Ayatollah Mohamed Bakr Al-Hakim's funeral are finally arriving. The procession numbers in the tens of thousands. The ayatollah was blown up by a massive car bomb while leaving Friday prayers here last week. It was a little like blowing up the pope in St. Peter's Square, and everyone's waiting to see who will take the blame.

Meanwhile, Seb is at the Baghdad Police Headquarters, where another bomb has just gone off. We've been taking bets on which hotel will be bombed first and fully expect them to start hitting civilian targets any time now. The mourners are marching through the streets, beating their breasts and shouting about revenge, and the American forces assigned to keep order are hanging way back. The supposedly disbanded Badr Brigade (the militia of the Supreme Council of the Islamic Revolution in Iraq, of which Al-Hakim was the spiritual leader) is providing security instead.

We try to follow the coffin to the shrine where Al-Hakim's brother Abdul-Aziz, the leader of the political wing of the SCIRI, will speak, but we are blocked by a pair of cops who can't believe a Westerner would be stupid enough to even consider going. Though I try and convince Ali, the translator I'm working with, to press the issue, he lets it drop, and we head back to Baghdad.

Baghdad
9.6.03

Kathleen is out of money, and we don't have enough to continue paying for everyone's room and board. The staff agreed a few weeks ago that they would have to freelance if the magazine wasn't making enough money. I didn't like this plan, but I liked the alternative even less. I conceded, hoping it wouldn't come to this, but it has.

We've run the magazine for four months with the twenty-five thousand dollars we received from Alistair and Dave, a British banker whom Ralph convinced to throw another ten thousand dollars at us in July. Advertising steadily increased in the weeks leading up to the U.N. bombing (we've even hired another ad man), but it still only covers about half of our costs—about four thousand dollars an issue. The difference between where we are and break-even is the price of a few international advertisements. We're in danger of running the mag into the ground if we continue like this. Right now we can afford to print the next issue, but we're going to lose one writer before that—Kathleen—and the realization makes me ill. Kathleen feels terrible. I've spent the entire evening trying to comfort her. She doesn't want to leave, but there's no choice. She has one hundred dollars left in the country, and Ralph has asked her to use it to pay for her share of the room and board. She has already called home in tears, and her mother calls back a few hours later, wanting to talk to me.

Kathleen offers to lie.

"You don't have to talk to her. I'll tell her you're asleep."

I have no idea what to say to Kathleen's mom, so I pick up the phone and listen. She's livid.

"Can you assure me my daughter is safe?"

"I will use my personal funds to make sure she can get out of the country," I say, knowing that doing so would leave me broke. I've already poured all the money I have into the magazine.

"What you're doing is irresponsible."

I can't disagree. She demands to talk to Ralph, and I wake him, put him on the phone, and go to the roof to smoke a cigarette. Half an hour later Ralph comes up.

"What are we going to do?"

"We have to stop printing. We can't run like this. How can we keep bringing people out in a situation like this? We can't pay Iraqis enough to find replacement writers, if we could even find people to hire."

We agree that I'll take the vacation I've planned on while Ralph stays in Iraq and maintains a small staff. We'll keep publishing on the Web until we figure out what to do. There are lots of people in the States, I figure, whom I can ask for money and support. I've already been talking to a few people. Twenty-five thousand dollars is less than the budget for most major magazine pieces.

A few days later Ralph, Catherine, Kathleen, and I leave for Jordan. Catherine needs to open a bank account in Amman, Kathleen's going back to the U.K., and Ralph needs money from our account in Amman to pay our bills.

Najaf
9.8.03

Before she leaves the country, Kathleen manages to set up a meeting with Moqtada Al-Sadr. She has been spending quite a bit of time reading about the Shia and building contacts within the community. Although Al-Sadr has met with reporters in recent weeks, the amount of press contact he has had is diminishing. His spokesman tells Kathleen the interview is an exclusive, and she's guardedly excited. The fact that we, a quickly failing news organization, have managed to score an exclusive quickly leads to discussions of how this coup can be exploited. In our haste I suggest that Kathleen contact some of the major newspaper offices in town and offer a story about Al-Sadr, which leads them to call his spokesman and complain. By the time the appointed date finally rolls around, we're part of a media convoy traveling to interview the reclusive cleric. Feras, who has demonstrated a frightening prescience about past attacks (at one point he dragged reporters off the street less than half an hour before a grenade attack), is afraid to go.

"What better target than a convoy of press?" he asks. Al-Sadr's supporters, he points out, have already been clashing with Coalition troops. "What better alibi could he have? He could attack the convoy himself."

It's a frightening notion, especially because we have to travel past Hilla, a small city about twenty miles south of Baghdad that has been the site of vicious drive-bys against aid workers and other nonmilitary foreign targets. Feras is suspiciously late on the morning of the interview, so we go with Salam. We make it to Najaf safely, and while we're waiting to be admitted to Al-Sadr's house I strike up a conversation with an Egyptian BBC journalist. I back into an admission that we don't have a translator with us, and she graciously agrees to help out.

We're admitted into a room adorned only with mats and a picture of Al-Sadr's father, a respected cleric who was murdered, most likely by Saddam, in 1998. Al-Sadr glares at me when I tell him I'm American, but he seems to take a liking to Kathleen. For better than half an hour he rants and raves, dancing around questions about the strength of his militia and what it would take for them to fight. He keeps slipping Kathleen something akin to a "come-hither" look.

I'm always impressed by the double standard toward Western women. On the streets in Najaf, if Kathleen's abbiya slips, a crowd of men will begin to follow her, shouting and threatening physical abuse until she rights the garment. Kathleen hates this. During one interview she even asks an ayatollah, one of the heads of a local political party, what he would do if one of his four daughters decided not to wear the abbiya. He simply smiled.

"That would never happen. It is her duty," he said.

In any case, Al-Sadr seems to find Kathleen attractive. It's still unclear how seriously we should be taking this guy, a wannabe ayatollah who swears he's thirty but who most people think is five years or so younger. The U.S. military in Najaf claims not to take him seriously and even suggests that he's stoned most of the time. But we see no evidence of that here, except for his efforts to convince Kathleen to become his envoy to Britain, which seems a fairly half-baked notion to me.

Iraqi/Jordanian Border
9.9.03

I lie and say we have flights from Amman tonight. Our car is near the end of a long line of vehicles trying to get over the border. The searches are thorough—each one takes about half an hour—and a number of people are being turned back, which further slows the process. The border guard ignores me at first, then shoots me a dirty look. There are at least a dozen other people here trying to get out of Iraq as soon as possible. A member of the Governing Council arrives, and the guards let him through immediately. After the rest of the crowd disperses, he tells Kathleen and me to get everyone else into our car and come get visas.

Lying rarely works: everyone seems to have a story, some reason they need to cross ahead of everyone else. Iraqis have also told us that Jordanian officials steal the visas of persons with dual citizenship, because their passports can be resold to people who need to leave Iraq under a different identity.

We pull our car to the front of the line and unpack everything for the guards. They flip through books, empty dirty laundry, disassemble Kathleen's saxophone, which we encourage her to reassemble and play. She does, briefly, and when she stops, no one acknowledges her, though a number of people have gathered to watch.

One of the guards finds a Kalashnikov clip in the console of the car. Nasir, the driver, says his kids put it there after he had taken it and the gun out. The guards empty the clip, one bullet at a time, and then replace the bullets. Nasir argues with them to return it, but they won't. We yell at him to give it up—we all just want to get out of Iraq. I don't realize it now, but I've already printed a fitting eulogy for the magazine in the last issue. We told everyone we would be back and the magazine would start printing again and Kathleen and I are the only ones who are planning to leave the country, but this will not be the case.

Baghdad Bulletin
9.1.03

"A letter from suburbia"
By Ihsan Charchafchi

Editor's note: Here at the Bulletin, *we have wrestled often with notions of cultural imperialism. To confuse us further, we recently received this letter from a friend of regular* Bulletin *contributor Youkhana Daniel. We sincerely hope Mr. Charchafchi (and please note, we only apply courtesy titles to those that fully lacerate us verbally) will continue to contribute.*

A few weeks ago I was told by a friend that an English paper is being published by British and Iraqi journalists in Baghdad. I tried in vain to obtain a copy of this paper, just to find out what an Englishman sitting in an air-conditioned office drinking German beer and smoking Indian cigars made without a license from Castro can tell us about the feelings of ordinary Iraqis towards the liberation (turned to an occupation by the orders of a U.N. resolution). No one in our neighborhood or in the book shops of the central part of the city sold the *Baghdad Bulletin.* I have been told that it is available in Saadun Street.

But why should I go to Saadun Street since we are spending the evenings in our suburban home enjoying the benefits of our newly acquired freedom (under the occupation), complete evenings spent watching the sky, breathing the natural fresh air and reading books about the merit of American capitalism using a replica of Aladdin's lamp. And when the CPA decides to be generous enough to give us electricity, there are six thousands channels at the tip of your finger telling you the depressing news in six hundred languages, or you can see your favorite movie with improved shoot-up sound effects.

When will I find the time to go to Saadun Street? We have been having a huge party, with lots of dancing, since April 9. Months of dancing in the streets, sorry that dear Donny couldn't make it to the party, probably he is busy drawing other plans for other countries.

I asked my dear friend Youkhana Daniel if he had seen the paper.

"Did I see it?" he said. "I write in it, and you can write in it too, they are looking for local writers."

"But if we can't get a copy it means that there is no one who reads it."

"Never mind who reads it," Youkhana replied. "They pay five cents per word, and that settled it as far as I am concerned." (Accounting department please note, the tally is $17.65 so far.)

As an Iraqi citizen, I'd like to address the CPA directly and talk frankly about our grievances: Hello? Hello? is there any body there? See? no answer, probably they are watching CNN or the BBC to find out what is happening in Iraq. Well, never mind, I will continue, since I am in it for the money as Mick Jagger keeps reminding us.

I am glad to express myself in the language of Shakespeare, Bob Dylan and the *Wall Street Journal*. But our education wouldn't be complete without learning the action-men English, the language of the movies, comics and the gangsters' talk. We wouldn't be cultured men till we use four letter words in our daily talk, and include such words as Jing-a-ling, Hotsi totsi, Honky-tonk. We need and demand to be educated.

So I am really thrilled to have you around to take our hands, we the noble savages and the not so noble savages of this world to a heaven of Kentucky-fried chickens, McDonalds and please don't forget the Coke. Take our hands and teach us how to use the computers, the Internet, how to cook accountant books and most important thing of all—how to be a successful fraud.

I am really pleased that you are staying around till we reorganize our government on the same moral standard in which your government is based (government of businessmen, by businessmen, and for businessmen).

Thank you for having me as a guest writer, and if you are going to pay me for this bull-shit (Account department please note bull-shit are two words), you are a greater sucker than I ever hoped for.

Vista, California
9.12.2003

When I arrive in California, there are already e-mails waiting for me. Angry ones from James. And slowly, after much prodding and cursing, apologetic ones from Ralph. Ralph, who while he was in Jordan went to the British and American embassies to tell them that Feras had offered to help him traffic weapons in order to raise money for the mag. It happened a few days before we left for Amman, Ralph says. Feras approached him, and it scared him so badly that he didn't want to tell me. He's sincere, but I still can't figure out why Feras would do something like that. So Ralph played along and went to Amman as planned, and grassed on Feras. I doubt the security officers at the embassies took him seriously, but I find out later that they were calling our house in Baghdad shortly thereafter. Ralph sent James a driver and a message to leave the country, but no explanation. James still doesn't know: Ralph won't tell him. He just keeps saying James is safer if he knows nothing about it.

I still can't believe it. Ralph must have gone nuts. I picture him sitting on the roof on one of Fadhil's nights off, wearing a flak jacket and sitting in a lawn chair with the Kalashnikov in his lap, pointed aimlessly out toward the neighborhood. I walk upstairs, laugh at the sight. He's got a beer on one side and a pack of cigarettes on the other side.

"What are you doing?"

"Guarding the house."

"All right, but I'm not taking a shift. I've got a lot of work to do."

But how nuts is he? There are other guys in the neighborhood, Iraqis, who do the same thing. Besides, I'm worried I've lost it as well. I know Lauren sees it. Sometimes I just get quiet; something she'll say will trigger something in my head, and I'll be thousands of miles away.

But I'm in California. There's nothing I can do now, and if I were there, the whole thing would probably have driven me over the edge. It's about seven A.M. here. I don't know all the details: Ralph pulled everyone out under cover of darkness, without even telling the Iraqi staff. The British embassy is calling our house in Baghdad. Other people are already telling me about threats against us in Baghdad, prices on our heads. I'm pretty sure these rumors are unfounded, but leaving town as we did is virtually guaranteed to make us look like spooks. Fortunately, as I find out later, all of our Iraqi staffers manage to find other jobs or return to their old ones, and the fact that Ralph pulled James overnight, without telling any of them, apparently has left them more or less safe from suspicion of anything more than unwitting involvement.

Mark and I have been trying to find buyers for the magazine, backers, anyone. He has written to George Soros, and I've scoured the American Left press—no one can take on a project of this magnitude. We've even talked to the Department for International Development (the British government's equivalent of USAID). They supplied half a million dollars to start a training program for Iraqi journalists, even though there's nowhere for them to work once they finish the program. But they're not interested either, despite having a lot of money left to spend.

A few potential investors have asked if we'd be willing to turn the *Bulletin* into a business magazine, catering to profiteers. I'm not.

Highway 101, California
9.15.2003

It's a near perfect day as Lauren and I drive up the coast toward Berkeley. I returned to the States a little less than a week ago, flying from Amman to Frankfurt to Los Angeles on September 11.

On this day two years ago I was in New York. Now I'm in California for the first time in my life, winding my way up the coast with a girlfriend who laughs when I jump at loud noises and doesn't bother me too much when I suddenly fall silent. Lauren's parents have been kind enough to lend us their big Ford pickup, and though normally I'd complain about driving something that uses so much gas, I appreciate the V8 engine and the surprising smoothness of the ride. After months of crashing around Baghdad in the passenger seats of crumpled taxicabs with no shocks, it feels good to drive. Lauren asks if I need a break, but I hate to relinquish the feeling of a steering wheel under my own control.

The Pacific is on our left, stretching out further than the road ahead, which already seems endless.

We're on our way to meet Daniel Ellsberg, at the invitation of a mutual friend whom I contacted while I was looking for support for the *Bulletin*. The friend couldn't offer much money but was able to arrange for me to meet a hero of mine, one of the bravest men in recent American history.

Ellsberg's house is a quiet little bungalow with a nice view in the hills above Berkeley. He invites us in and apologizes for eating while we talk—he hasn't had time for lunch.

We talk about the farcical invasion and the disastrous occupation. Ellsberg is eager for firsthand information. He had been planning to make a trip to Iraq some months ago but was discouraged by the long and potentially dangerous car ride over the border. Bad for his back, he says.

He is still keen and angry, but it's that good kind of anger, the kind that comes from finally understanding what people are capable of, the damage they'll inflict upon one another when following orders.

The conversation ambles on for a few hours. As Lauren and I thank Ellsberg and prepare to leave, I decide to ask the question that I've been dying to ask for a long time. I'm not sure how he'll take it, but we've been talking about the helplessness we all feel in the face of the war machine, so I figure it's okay to ask.

"How do you keep going?"

"I think we'll all be rounded up and put in camps. I'm an old man, and I figure I'll die in a camp."

November 2003

Grand Rapids, Michigan
10.22.03

This is it. Last night in Grand Rapids before I go back. I hate good-byes. I went to a party a few nights ago and ended up in front of the house with a girl I knew from high school and a Vietnam vet. He talked about his war, about the killings he saw, about My Lai and the others that were just like it but failed to become household names. I don't know if he was telling the truth, but he started crying, and there I was, standing on the sidewalk with a man I had never met before, and he just started crying. Maybe he was just drunk.

Imagine having a front-row seat to the new world order and not even knowing it. Most Iraqis will never have a chance to meet the occupation officials whose decisions now govern their lives. They will just be stuck accepting the new rules, and the first rule is that the victor makes the rules.

At the *Bulletin* we received dozens of open letters to "President Bush," "Commander Bush," "The Honorable Mr. Bush." They came from eight-year-olds and professionals and everyone in between.

Dear Mr. Bush—

This is a letter from an Iraqi woman who lived in the United States for 10 years, and I enjoyed every minute of it. I am so grateful for the American people who helped me and my husband get our doctorates in your country. I always think of the States as my second home, and if I had the choice to go back and enjoy the freedom and the democracy your country enjoys, I would.

The reason I'm writing to you sir is to give you a picture of what's going on in my country since you came to free it from the regime of Saddam Hussein. My family and I were against the regime from its start, and it got worse year after year. He put me in jail for five years, from 1991 to 1996. I spent one of them in the Iraqi Intelligence Department, a cell in which it was too dark to see my hand in front of my face. I could not see my family—all for disagreeing with his son-in-law, Hussein Kamel, while I was a director general in the Issue Department of the Central Bank of Iraq.

After my release I joined the Al-Mansur University, a private university, to avoid becoming reinvolved with the government. All this time, we have been waiting to be freed from sanctions and from the regime, but even though it has happened, I have not had a moment to enjoy it.

Things have begun to get worse for my country. I would love to see security and the order restored to the Iraqi society. People are dreaming of a decent life with a good infrastructure, with good communication. The heat in my country reaches 55 degrees Centigrade in the shade. With no electric power, just imagine the elderly and the children suffering in the heat.

There is no trash collection, the water is dirty and sewerage systems are not working. And on top of it, we are forced to spend hours in line to be searched for weapons. Why did they let people loot the weapons? Now they want them back.

I am a mother and a wife and my heart is bleeding to see these people suffering from unemployment. Not every Iraqi is from the Baath Party, so why are they out of their jobs? We have a saying in Iraq sir, "hunger is murder."

My heart is bleeding for your soldiers, too, and I hate to see them being hurt and killed by my people. I don't want to see another Vietnam.

I want them to remember Iraq as a great civilization that taught the world to read and write.

So please, Mr. Bush, by all the mercy of all the religions in the world, try to help the women of Iraq, mothers, sisters, wives, to have a decent life for their families.

This letter was dictated to me by Maysoon, an economics professor. She cried as she spoke; one thing she did not mention in the letter was that she was tortured repeatedly in prison. We received dozens of letters similar to this one, some more articulate than others. We began referring to them as "Letters to Santa Claus."

Baghdad
11.24.03

When was the last time you were walking through your neighborhood and saw a tank run over a car?

It was no one's fault. It happened on Karrada Street, a busy but normally peaceful shopping district. A normal traffic accident—the car in front of the tank stalled, and the tank ran over it. The driver was lucky. He managed to slide far enough to the side that only his legs were crushed. Incidents like this are so common that the United States has already doled out millions of dollars in compensation.

I've come back to Baghdad to freelance and to work for Occupation Watch, an NGO that monitors the effects of the occupation and advocates for a full Coalition withdrawal. I'm reporting for them, but other staffers are helping people like Antoine Nooruddin, whose son was killed by U.S. troops, file claims against the military. Antoine's claim has been turned down. He's unsurprised. He knew the odds were against him.

"Well, what can we do?" he says, putting his head in his hands. I'm sitting in his living room with Paola, an Italian woman who works with Occupation Watch through another NGO. She's spent the last few months cataloging deaths caused by the U.S. military and helping Iraqis file for the meager compensation payments that are available. It usually goes poorly.

Antoine has been visiting one U.S. military office after another for nearly four months. His thirty-eight-year-old son, Mazen, was shot and killed by soldiers from the First Armored Division on June 28 as he waited for a taxi near his home in Dora, a southern suburb. Mazen was riddled with bullets fired by a U.S. soldier in response to a machine gun attack coming from a location more than one hundred feet away from where he was standing. A two-hundred-foot-wide swath of bullet holes is still evident on walls and houses along the road. It's Paola who brings Antoine the letter from the military, informing him compensation has been denied because Mazen was killed in a "combat situation."

It's amazing no one else was killed—.50-cal bullets ended up inside almost every house along the stretch.

The trip through the claims process is a terrible odyssey: endless paperwork and innumerable visits to Coalition offices are more often than not rewarded with a letter of ineligibility, thanks to the elasticity of the "combat situation" rule. Lawyers at the Civil Military Operation Centers often accept claims only one day a week. Long waits and delays are the norm, and it is not uncommon for files to be lost, so that the whole process must be started from scratch.

Paola and other activists have found the military often will not accept claims from Iraqis unless they are accompanied by foreigners. My Iraqi friends have a joke about situations that work like that. Their solution to dealing with them is to "rent a whitey"—i.e., borrow one of us to come with them to make sure they get fair treatment.

The payments, when they are made, are usually twenty-five hundred dollars or less, and they come with the caveat that the claim can no longer be pursued. The claims are awarded by military lawyers who are charged with investigating each case, but often they do little more than contact the commanding officer of the unit for a report.

"I don't know what else you could do. The first principle of the process is that it's a gratuitous process. There's nothing in international law that requires us to have a claims process," one of the military lawyers says when I ask him if it seems reasonable to have the army conduct its own investigations in these matters. There is a line of more than eighty people outside his office, some who have made long drives to be there. People leave his office shouting so often that he has become used to it.

"The solace payments were much higher in Bosnia—I think it was twenty-five thousand dollars," he says, though he admits he doesn't know why. I'm still amazed he's so young, in his mid-twenties. People often chide me for looking young, but this kid is in charge of putting a value on people's lives.

"In America would they be able to pay twenty-five hundred dollars when they kill someone? I think the settlement would be more than one million dollars," says a man waiting outside who is trying to reclaim property he says is now part of a U.S. military base.

In Mazen's case the soldiers initially gave statements that he was in the car with the men who attacked them. Paola and Ismael, an Iraqi human rights activist, found and interviewed a number of Iraqi witnesses to disprove this.

The troops also took Mazen's body to the airport with them. When his father went to the airport to request that it be returned to the family, Antoine Nooruddin was told he would have to take Mazen's body back from the airport in a taxi. When he complained that no taxi would pick him up, troops grudgingly drove him from the airport to the end of his street but were too scared to go further. Men from the neighborhood helped him carry his son's body the rest of the way. Despite all the humiliation and pain, Nooruddin still doesn't resent the American presence. He's glad that Saddam is gone. But Mazen was the main earner in the family. Antoine is seventy-two, and his wife is ailing.

"In 1991 we had to sell everything," says Antoine, who worked for thirty-three years at the same airport where he went to find his son's body. He has traveled all over Europe and to America and makes pleasant conversation in English, remembering better times, but always turmoil. He has a lot of stories to tell. As a young man, he happened to be on Haifa Street, buying a newspaper, when Saddam Hussein attempted to assassinate Abdul Karim Qassim, the prime minister, in 1959. He saw Saddam run away from the scene of the crime. I'm trying to picture what a parade on Haifa Street would look like. For me it's only a place of desolation and bombs placed in the median. A place of giant state-owned apartment buildings and dangerous back alleyways, a place that was dangerous enough to force the British embassy out of their historic colonial residence and into the Green Zone. "I had money, but then the Iraqi dinar went down in value after 1991."

Now the family's only source of income is the U.S. Army: the only job Mazen's brother can find is as an army translator. He is fortunate. Most of the men in the neighborhood don't have jobs at all. The troops were scared for a reason. Dora is a site of frequent attacks, nasty ones. Guerillas lie in wait under bridges. The base near here is mortared often.

"There is a grave next to Mazen's with a mother and her two sons," Antoine says. "They were shot because they didn't stop at a checkpoint. They probably did not understand the command."

Baghdad
11.26.03

The occupation's marketing team must have no sense of irony. Or maybe they have a truly brutal sense of it and are hoping that everyone else gets the message. The signage that has been appearing at roadsides and on rooftops is becoming more and more comical. One billboard offers a twenty-five-hundred-dollar reward for tips leading to the capture of resistance fighters. It pictures a tough-looking Iraqi police officer. Behind him a group of U.S. troops is subduing a man.

Most of these billboards are either covered with paint or shot up within a few days of their debut. In Al-Adamiyah they are always defaced by the next morning. I like the billboards that wish everyone a happy Ramadan, but even those carry an implicit message about who's in charge. We say you can have a happy Ramadan, so go right ahead, hajji.

Baghdad
11.27.03

Dinner with Feras. I'm not really sure what to do, but I've called him, and he's going to pick me up in a few minutes. I figure it's fine. A neutral place, we'll talk about families and girlfriends, shoot the breeze.

We go to Mataam Shamse, one of the omnipresent campy pizza places. Bright décor, music videos on a television perched in the corner of the dining room, young men and women out to eat in groups, in couples, and narguilehs as the night winds down and the patrons begin to thin.

Feras knows I want to ask. He hints at it.

"Why did Ralph leave?"

"I'm not sure."

"He didn't say anything about it? We were very surprised."

"Well, he did say one thing."

Feras reiterates the offer to me.

"We can make almost five hundred thousand dollars on one shipment," he says.

I put my head on the table and try to laugh. He offers a cigarette and I take it, and then we sit there and both laugh. I haven't seen him since.

Abu Ghraib Prison
11.28.03

They've renamed it the Baghdad Correctional Facility, but things are very much the same as before. The family members of those detained inside wait anxiously in front of the prison gate, standing in line for hours hoping for news of their loved ones. The road from the visitors' parking lot is a humiliating and muddy slog, but lawyers and family make the trek every day, only to be met at the gate by U.S. military police, who tell them that only twenty visits are allowed each day. Two days out of the week are for lawyers only.

"They told me to come back in four months," says one man as he walks away from the prison. "My son has already been in there for four months, and he has been charged with nothing! It was easier to get a visit under Saddam!"

I'm here with Rory, a Scottish filmmaker. We've come to the prison in search of Rory's friend Yunis, a cameraman who was arrested during a raid on his house in the north Baghdad neighborhood of Al-Adamiyah.

A chunky military policeman ignores the Iraqis who approach the gate with us and speaks directly to Rory and me, a pair of Westerners.

"How do we request a visit with a prisoner?" Rory asks.

"Do you have the prisoner's number?"

"Yes."

The MP looks surprised. It's impossible to get a visit without knowing the prisoner's number, which can be almost impossible to obtain. Either arresting soldiers fail to provide it, or the military fails to include it on the lists they distribute to Iraqi offices, and names are misspelled during capture and cataloging. Without a number, a family can't even begin to guess where their relative might be held. Yunis's family obtained his and his brothers' numbers when a neighbor detained in the same camp was released. Before his release he wrote down the numbers and locations of the men he knew. This is how the fortunate families find their detained relatives, from numbers scrawled on scraps of cloth torn from prison-yard tents.

"You can stand in line with everyone else and wait to fill out a form," the MP says.

More than one hundred people are already in line, and it is only ten A.M. For many this is a daily vigil. Some are unsure whether their friends and family are even here: they are simply hoping to match a name with a recorded prisoner. About one hundred more people are in the parking lot, and still more are just arriving. Only one translator is working the gate; the other one hasn't turned up for work today.

The MP notices that I'm writing down everything he says.

"Are you journalists?" he asks.

"Well, yes. But I'm just trying to find out about my mate," Rory replies.

Yunis worked in a hotel before the invasion and as a part-time journalist and began working with Rory in April. He was in Rory's employ when he was arrested. Rory shows me footage of Yunis conducting interviews with eyewitnesses to Richard Wild's murder back in July—a more thorough investigation than that conducted by the Coalition forces.

The family suspects Yunis was arrested because he had been making frequent filming trips to Faluja, the site of strong anti-American resistance. Khraymer, Yunis's father, says one of the neighbors probably told the Americans about his son's visits to Faluja. Informants are paid by the military, which often acts without investigating the reliability of the intelligence. Of course, in some cases the tipsters are simply settling grudges. In June nearly four hundred men were arrested in one such operation in Dhuloiya, a village about forty kilometers north of Baghdad. All were eventually released. The father of the man whose tip allegedly sparked the raid killed his own son in order to prevent the other men of the village from doing so. In some cases, Iraqis have told me that troops have even apologized for arresting them on bad intelligence or have told them who provided the tip that led to their arrest.

Khraymer's oldest son, Iass, was detained with his brothers but is released after spending three days in a Baghdad police station. In the box for "reason for arrest" on his arrest ticket is written "planning assassination of Tony Blair." Other released detainees have complained of similar accusations. It appears to be an accident that Iass was allowed to keep his arrest ticket after his release. He assumes the charge was a joke, but no one finds it funny.

"You need to go to the 800th MP division to get permission to be here," the MP says. "You need an escort."

The MP gives me the phone number of an officer I've already e-mailed, requesting information about the prison. That officer said he couldn't help me. His unit had ceded control of the prison to the CPA a week before.

Not needing to confirm whether our friend is being held here—a confirmation that many of the families lined up here need before they can even fill out a visit request—we turn and begin the muddy slog back to the parking lot. The MP looks down at a small boy, about seven years old, whose father is inside.

"You need to smile more," he tells the boy.

Yunis, along with his brothers Abbass and Khalid, are three of the more than ten thousand detainees the CPA admits to holding, though many suspect the real number is no less than twice that. Virtually all are being detained indefinitely and without charges as "suspected terrorists." All the families assembled at Abu Ghraib say their relatives are innocent, picked up in indiscriminate raids conducted on bad information. They have little evidence to back up their claims; but given the rumors about people showing up at the prison to visit relatives and being arrested themselves, it seems hard to believe that anyone would show up if they truly believed their relatives were guilty. Some of those proclaiming innocence admit that they're frightened. It's common for the Americans to raid all of the houses belonging to an extended family, or to arrest all of the brothers from a single family.

For Yunis's family the raid came early on the morning of September 23. Troops landed on the roof of the house from helicopters and came in through an upstairs door, while others below ordered Khraymer to unlock his front door.

"Then they handcuffed me and took my sons," Khraymer

says. "They also took five million [Iraqi] dinars [about twenty-five hundred dollars]." Khraymer says the soldiers gave no reason for the arrests. They returned the next day to inform him that his house was suspected of being a center for bomb-making and counterfeiting, although they admitted that no equipment for either purpose had been found.

Khraymer said the confiscated dinars included about twenty thousand in counterfeit notes. This is not unusual. A large amount of counterfeit notes is believed to be in circulation.

The dual financial blow dealt to the family in losing their main breadwinners and a large sum of money is far overshadowed by the sense of personal loss.

Many of the families have traveled to multiple prisons across the country, searching for news. The trip from the detention facility in Tikrit, in the north, to Camp Bucca in Umm Qasr, in the south, takes eleven hours by car, and prisoners are moved frequently. Transliterated names, often spelled incorrectly, can make things even harder. "Look at us—all of us know at least three people who are detained," says Jihad Abbass, who traveled from Faluja in search of news about his five sons, ages sixteen to twenty-two. They were arrested in a raid on his house on the night of his eldest son's wedding, in July. A crowd of about forty men surrounds Jihad Abbass in the visitor's parking lot, telling similar tales of houses raided, valuables taken, and long searches for news, sometimes not knowing whether their relatives are dead or alive.

Though visits are technically allowed, their actual number is exceedingly small, and the process requires that families have access to a lawyer. The military has said there is a process by which all detainees can receive legal counsel, but interviews with released detainees call this claim into question. The technical requirement to provide counsel is stymied by delays in the approval process and a strict limit on the number and frequency of visits. We cannot find a single released detainee who says he received access to counsel. The International Committee of the Red Cross, the only organization authorized to monitor conditions in the detention camps, has drastically reduced its presence since a car bombing of its Baghdad headquarters in September. The ICRC's effectiveness was in question well before that, however. In June an ICRC employee in Baghdad told me there were camps within the country to which even the Red Cross did not have access. Written contact that the ICRC facilitated between detainees and their families seems to have trailed off around June. Some families said that before that they had been receiving messages or letters every fifteen days.

All fear the worst when their relatives are detained. One man said he went to Abu Ghraib and was told that his son had died in custody, but no one had notified the family. Reportedly, the translator who delivered the terrible news was then reprimanded by a nearby American commander, who warned the translator that he should have told the man his son had been "released."

There have been numerous unconfirmed reports of hunger strikes and prisoner demonstrations. The CPA admitted that four prisoners were killed and eight wounded during a November 24 uprising at Abu Ghraib. I don't know this at the time, but Yunis was one of the leaders of the uprising. All of the prisoners in his camp (Abu Ghraib is divided into eight different tent camps, plus the existing prison buildings) refused to go back to their tents after evening prayers. It was the last day of Ramadan, and they said they had been repeatedly promised by prison guards that they would be released in time to spend Eid Al-Fitr, the feast that marks the end of a month of fasting, with their families. That won Yunis and three other men elected as prisoner representatives in the camp's informal social system a meeting with one of the commanders at the camp. They demanded better treatment—it was cold and they did not have enough blankets, prisoners were denied medical attention, prisoners were taken from the camp to be tortured—they wanted it to stop. The commander, Yunis tells me later, said he could do nothing.

"Then I cannot be held responsible for the actions of these

men," Yunis told him before returning to the camp. What followed is related in a hygienic military press release:

> Prisoners at BCF began throwing rocks at the military police guarding the gates as well as those in the guard towers. Initially, soldiers were instructed to use non-lethal rounds to try to quell the disturbance, however the riot escalated to other compounds and lethal force was authorized. The uprising was under control in about 10 minutes. Three detainees were killed during the riot and eight were wounded. The wounded prisoners were air evacuated to a nearby medical facility.
>
> The cause of the incident is yet unknown. The escalation in the use of force was based on the situation and conditions of the incident.

Rory and I go to Yunis's house for the Eid. It is normally a festive event, but for many this year it is subdued, especially in Al-Adamiyah.

Yunis's mother hurries from the room as his father, Khraymer Abbass Salman, tells the story of the raid in which his sons were arrested. She cannot hear it without breaking into tears.

"I tell my children their father is traveling, but they don't believe me," Abbass's wife says. She says she doesn't know how her husband could have been suspected of being a member of the resistance, as he is a medical doctor with two young children. His brother Khalid is twenty-one. He will lose an entire year of study if he isn't released soon. As for Yunis, the lost dinars were to be used for his upcoming wedding. The family is in touch with his fiancée, who says she will wait for him. But we all wonder how long it will be.

December 2003

Diwaniya

12.4.03

Today is Jesus Suarez's son Eric's second birthday. Eric's grandfather Fernando Suarez del Solar will mark the day by visiting the place where Jesus, a U.S. marine, was killed on March 27 after stepping on a modified bomb, an American DPICM (Dual Purpose Improved Conventional Munition), the kind that break into eighty-eight smaller fragments on impact. He was guarding the perimeter of his platoon's encampment.

The place where Jesus was killed is in view of Highway 1, which connects Baghdad to the southern city of Basra: a desolate, muddy stretch of land. The earth is still churned from the heavy military machinery that passed through months ago on the way to Baghdad. The only landmarks are a cement factory and a destroyed Republican Guard camp. Camels pass by as Fernando makes his way out to the site. The international press slogs along behind him. Everyone is looking out for unexploded bombs. Fernando plants a crucifix and collects some earth from the spot before he collapses.

Bob Woodruff, a correspondent for ABC News, was embedded with Jesus's regiment for a month. He has brought Fernando to this place, and sits next to him atop a small mound of earth while he reads his notes from the night when Jesus was killed. Woodruff stops for the passing U.S. convoys, waiting until he can be heard again. A pile of mortar casings, detritus from Jesus's platoon, lies nearby.

" 'Suarez, keep your eyes open,' the medics tell him," Woodruff reads. "They are asking him about his wife, where he is from. . . . The chopper that is supposed to take him to the field hospital never comes—it has broken down, but they do not tell us this."

Woodruff moves a few days ahead in his notes, to Jesus's funeral.

"The innocence and bravado of his platoon is gone. One after another, Suarez's friends kneel before his helmet, his gun, and his boots."

Fernando has come from Escondido to lead a delegation of American veterans and military families who want to see the realities of occupied Iraq for themselves. Their message is clear—bring the troops home.

The group spends the week meeting with various Coalition officials, Iraqi dignitaries, and ordinary citizens, and, in the case of those who still have family members serving here, attempting to visit them. They're shocked by the kilometer-long petrol queues that form every night in anticipation of the stations' opening the following morning and heartened to experience the increasing vibrancy of Baghdad's streets, which American news channels do not convey particularly effectively.

The delegation is scheduled to meet with Iraqis who lost relatives during or after the invasion, including the family of Mohaned Al-Kabi, the Coalition-appointed head of the Sadr City municipal council, who was shot in the back by a U.S. soldier last month.

"The American soldiers don't value the lives of the Iraqi people," says Hani Al-Kabi, Mohaned's brother. "My brother quit his job abroad as an engineer to help the people here, and they killed him."

The delegates walk a fine line between supporting the troops and standing in some sort of solidarity with bereaved Iraqis.

"It's too much—I see today five, six, seven different stories, and I know there are thousands," Fernando says, after spending a morning meeting with cluster-bomb victims. "The boy yesterday who lost his hand. If my son had survived, he could be like that—without a hand, without his sight.

"They are boys, they are victims," Fernando says of the marines. "They enter the marines for the opportunity to go to school, not for war. They want to finish their contract and get out.

"I was a social activist in Tijuana, and he saw the problems with children on drugs in Mexico," Fernando says. In 1997, when Jesus was fifteen, Fernando moved his family to the United States because Jesus wanted to join one of the army's antidrug units. He decided to start out in the marines. Sitting in the Al-Kabi family's living room, Fernando describes his son as a warrior for good to Mohaned's family.

"He just wanted to help children here," he tells them.

Mohaned's father explains the history of resistance in his tribe and in Sadr City.

"In 1920 my grandfather kicked the British out," the old man says, a fist in the air. "In 1958 we revolted against the king. Soon all Iraqis will revolt against the occupier."

I'm trying to figure out what the Americans in the room are thinking—they've just arrived after a daylong drive across the desert from Amman, which they began less than four hours after getting off their flight, which arrived at three A.M. local time. Now they're sitting in a living room in Sadr City, being told things are just kicking off.

Some try to argue that the American soldiers stationed here are only trying to do good. This doesn't last too long before they realize they need to shut up and listen.

Baghdad
12.14.03

It's around two o'clock in the afternoon when the firing starts. Sustained, loud. Paola and I are in the Occupation Watch office, and I grab my camera and run outside. The gunfire is coming from all directions, and the reports seem random, disorganized, not in response to each other.

"I bet they caught him," I say to Paola. "What else could it be?"

We step into the lobby of a nearby hotel, where people are crowded around a television showing old footage of Saddam. The newscaster says the fugitive leader has been captured. We decide to hit the street and start talking to people, but the first taxi driver we find gives us an earful.

"I waited for five hours today to get fuel," he says. "I was an architect before the invasion. What we need now is petrol, and people need food. It was better under Saddam."

We head over to New Baghdad, a mixed, lower-middle-class neighborhood with tight streets and a market on the main drag that spills out into the street.

"We are happy for not having Saddam anymore, maybe now the bomb attacks will stop," says Nizar Jabar Saad as he pays for a juice with a 250-dinar note bearing the newly arrested leader's face. "But the Iraqi people from east to west refuse the occupation."

"Saddam hurt the Iraqi people since the war with Iran, when he killed our brothers. My brother died during the most recent war," says a local shopkeeper. "But we want the justice and the life the Americans promised. Catching Saddam will not make the resistance go away. Providing people with food and electricity and security will make it go away."

Disbelief is widespread.

"They've arrested so many on the list of fifty-five, but where are they? Why won't they show us where they are?" asks a woman in the juice shop. "He should be tried in an Iraqi court, because he is guilty of crimes inside Iraq," she adds.

In Al-Adamiyah my friend Hamid, weeping, incites a demonstration. The protest swells as a crowd of anguished people fills the streets, carrying grenade launchers, Kalashnikovs, and heavier machine guns. Some have even strapped on suicide-bomb belts. By nightfall the celebrations in other neighborhoods have largely stopped, but the crowd in Al-Adamiyah has grown to more than one thousand They chant.

"B'il rouh! Biddam . . ."

"Would you be happy if there were Iraqis occupying the U.S. and they captured George W. Bush?" Hamid asks. As if to underscore the confusion, a journalist who has been working with Hamid points out that in May, Hamid (who is Shia) professed to hate Saddam.

"I'm not mad because they captured Saddam, but because they put another Iraqi in prison," he says.

The capture rends Iraqi society. In predominately Shiite areas, the mosques crow with a joyous "allahu akbar." In predominately Sunni areas like Al-Adamiyah, people recall the 1991 intifada, during which Shiites in the south, encouraged to revolt against Saddam, killed an unknown number of Sunni soldiers and officers.

"I was in Najaf in 1991 when the uprising began," Hamid says. "I was just a kid, and it was scary—I am ashamed to be a Shiite because of it."

Many Iraqis see little point in going out into the street after the news is announced.

"My problem is not to catch Saddam; it's not something important for me," says Hanna, a women's rights activist at Occupation Watch. Hanna's family is from Al-Owja, the Tikrit suburb where Saddam was born. "The struggle between Bush and Saddam is not my struggle, my struggle is against Bush and Saddam. Bush and Saddam are the same face—they are the face of Hitler. My problem is how must I go to peace and how must I go to justice."

For U.S. soldiers the capture is something to cheer about, but from a purely practical standpoint little will change.

"He's been out of the picture for so long, except for that one dinky little video earlier this year," says Sergeant Rachel Brune of the 800th MP Division. "When they made the official announcement of his confirmed capture—we were watching it on CNN—a cheer went up at our headquarters. . . . When you have a regime like this that was basically a cult of personality, and then you catch that personality, one can't help but think that a definitive blow has been dealt to the old regime."

Al-Dur
12.18.03

We've been trying for a week to get into the house where Saddam Hussein was captured. Hamid figured a beat-up old minibus would be inconspicuous, so he hired a driver named Mahmoud to take us north. Three trips up to Tikrit (a two-hour ride each way, with the option of lunch in Samarra), only to be told by the public affairs officer who ambles out of the base after a two-hour wait that there's no media access today.

"Dangg-itttt! I've forgotten the number for the major again! Sorry about that, I've really got to memorize that," is the last thing he says each time, before loping back into the base.

Not to say that there aren't things to be learned from spending two hours standing outside a choice target like this one. If anything happens, we'll be caught right between the shooting and a wide swath of return fire.

Uzma, a British activist who has come along for the ride, chats up a Lebanese contractor who's also waiting to be escorted inside. He provides prefab housing units and other support services to the military—a KBR competitor. We start talking about the economy.

"It's picking up. We've created six thousand jobs in Baghdad," he says.

Unemployment is currently estimated at 8.5 million.

"But what are they going to do when the military leaves?"

"Well . . . the economy is picking up."

"In which sectors? There are a lot of consumer goods being imported and not much else going on."

"Was the Israeli occupation a good thing for Lebanon's economy?" I ask quickly, breaking in for the first time.

"Well . . ."

Uzma immediately lays into him.

"Don't you feel like you're selling people out?"

"The way I see it is that I'm just making money. Doing my job. That's all I'm here to do. Make money."

The contractor also mentions that KBR doesn't hire Iraqis to drive trucks. Instead, they import third-country laborers and pay them $125,000 a year. He mentions that 40 percent of the KBR employees have quit, and many of them have started sub-contracting on their own at higher rates.

The argument starts to get out of control, so Uzma and I decide to make our own way up to the site. Troops in ghilly suits are patrolling the streets of Tikrit, backed by heavy armor. Two of them stand at alert in front of a sweet shop, fake foliage on their heads, presumably guarding a precious supply of Iraqi candies. The residents walk on past, continuing their shopping.

The soldiers look like aliens who don't know where they've landed. It's even better when they deploy from the armored personnel carriers. The jet engine turns off, and the hatch on the back of the APC slowly lowers, a mechanized process that takes a practically interminable thirty seconds. The soldiers pile out in full gear: night-vision goggles, guns at the ready. If they were in any real trouble, they'd have been attacked in the half minute it took the hatch to open.

The Americans are trailed by recruits from the new Iraqi Army, which is being trained and deployed under U.S. supervision. A few Iraqis on the street stop to shout at them.

"Take pictures of the monkeys!" they tell me.

The ICDC soldiers (the force has already been granted an acronym) scan the crowd nervously. Some wear balaklavas to cover their faces. ICDC troops (many of whom, in the current deployment, are not actually from Tikrit) are beginning to die as frequently as their American comrades.

We pick up some kebabs, figuring we'll take them to the troops standing guard at the perimeter of the house, or at least have a good piss trying. Feeling generous, I even pitch in for some Pepsis.

The house is surrounded by farms and orchards, dotted with the occasional shepherd or grazing cow. It's flat, and the mud is quite thick—November to January is winter in Iraq, which means lots of rain. Our kebabs are politely rebuffed by the American guards. We sheepishly offer them to the Iraqi soldiers, who share oranges with us. They say they found Saddam sitting in a hole beneath a small house in an orange grove. The Americans tell us to go home because they've been fired on here during the past few nights. If we come back first thing in the morning, they'll take us in. Fair enough.

"We don't actually know why the hell we're out here," says a soldier from the Fourth Infantry Division as we turn to leave. "What are they going to do with this place?"

Two hours back to Baghdad, with a detour near Balad to look for a house that Uzma can't find in the dark. She's stayed with a family there before, members of the resistance.

The next morning we show up just behind a convoy of reporters going to see the house. We're being given the grand tour. Amid bored-looking soldiers and a shoving crowd of journalists, the commander launches into a solemn description of "Operation Guard Saddam's Hole."

"Excuse me? Mr. Enders?"

I turn to find a sergeant standing over me. Literally. He must be at least six-six.

"You weren't invited."

Okay. That's a bad start.

"I'm sorry?"

"Can I see your press credential?"

"I'm working for the *Sunday Times.*"

"Can I see your press credential?"

"You can call London and confirm it."

"You don't work for an impartial organization, Mr. Enders."

I have a press credential, but it says "Occupation Watch" on it. Works for Iraqi stuff. I don't have any credentials the army has to honor because they don't have to honor anything. Feeling like an idiot, I realize that I sent this guy an e-mail on behalf of Occupation Watch a few weeks back. No wonder he hasn't been responding to my requests for a visit to the house. What's his name?

"I'm Master Segeant Cargie. You can take my name."

On the mistaken assumption this was something that could be solved reasonably, I've let Cargie walk me away from the house and the other journalists as we've talked. He suddenly turns away, up the deeply rutted road to the house.

"Find your own way back."

I briefly question whether he really thinks he's left me stranded before starting up a conversation with some of the 4ID guys standing guard nearby. I curse myself for not putting up a fight, making Cargie remove me bodily in front of the *Times* photographers. It probably wouldn't have done much good.

I can still hear his words: "You don't work for an impartial organization, Mr. Enders."

Master Sergeant, what is an impartial organization? Is the Armed Forces Network an impartial organization? Who still has any impartiality? Everyone covers stage-managed attempts to spin things the right way. A recent front-page article in the *Times,* dateline Tikrit: "When a reporter and a photographer for *The New York Times* walked into The Inn, apprehensively, it was a relief to be invited to sit down." I was walking around by myself on the streets of Tikrit a day or two earlier. I also had lunch, but hey, I thought it was just lunch. I was hungry. I was invited to sit down, too, and even to pay for my meal like everyone else.

It goes on and on and on: Bush shows up with a turkey for the troops (it was a prop used for photo ops); Rumsfeld flies in to talk up how good things look from the window of his heavily armed helicopter; the occupation government organizes a pro-American demo complete with schoolchildren carrying pictures of Ahmed Chalabi and protection from helicopters and sharpshooters. Al-Iraqia, the CPA-sponsored television station, which often reruns nature shows and dubbed Japanese movies to fill giant gaps in its programming, managed four hours of live coverage. I don't think anyone was fooled, except maybe the troops.

All of the Governing Council members have adopted the language of "fighting terrorism." It's a veritable Baghdad Vichy. The cops are dying as often as the troops, and the troops no longer trust the cops because they won't turn in resistance fighters who live in their neighborhoods. Iraqi recruits have begun resigning from the ICDC. Sixty dollars a month won't buy people willing to serve as surrogate targets. Under these circumstances, the truth can be hard to find.

Back at Saddam's house, a soldier who has been standing closer to the house walks out to the detachment I'm standing with. He's trying to light a cigar, a box of which have apparently been distributed to some of the 4ID guys nearby.

"Aren't you the guy Master Sergeant just kicked out of here?"

"Yeah."

"Well, why don't you leave?"

"I would, but Master Sergeant failed to kick out the driver and translator that came with me."

A few minutes later the Master Sergeant escorts Hamid and Mahmoud out. Mahmoud has managed to pick about half a dozen oranges.

"I wish I had known Saddam was here," he says, grinning broadly. "I would have come and picked him up and taken him out of the country."

The last picture on Hamid's camera is of a very angry-looking Sergeant Cargie, facing the lens, hands on hips, a little surprised by the flash. He's standing in front of the house where

Saddam apparently cooked Spaghetti-O's and whiled away the hours until his capture, pretending he wasn't Saddam and smiling contentedly to himself.

Al-Owja
12.16.03

After being rebuffed on our second trip to the base, we go to Al-Owja, Saddam's birthplace, instead. The town is entirely encircled in barbed wire. The soldiers at the checkpoint laughingly take our IDs and keep them, ensuring that we'll travel out the same way we came in.

The streets are deserted. There are three shops open, and a few children run about on a largely deserted playground. It's not much fun here, and the troops know it.

"Not much happens here anymore. We pretty much sealed off the town a couple months ago."

"We got this one guy. We call him the mortarman. He runs to somewhere over there [gesturing at empty brown fields] and shoots off a couple mortars and then runs away."

"He's done it so many times we just decided to call him the mortarman."

One of the guys just arrived from Afghanistan. The other is from Wisconsin. He has picked up a little Arabic.

"Tafteesh!"

The ICDC recruit smoking a cigarette nearby obediently stands up to search the man the soldier has stopped.

A trio of kids, no older than eight, come out toward the checkpoint and begin shouting "Long live Saddam!" at the soldiers. The soldier from Wisconsin walks a few steps toward them.

"Stop that!"

Laughing, the children turn and run away.

"Can't have them doing that," the soldier says.

"Why not?" Uzma asks him.

"Because it's been outlawed."

The men at one of the shops stand around us. They have little to say. Al-Owja is a small town, about eleven hundred people. A few hundred have been arrested. The rest have left. They don't know how many have been killed.

"Things have been real quiet here lately," one of the soldiers says. "Say, you guys got any newspapers? We ain't read a newspaper in months. Someone brought one up a few days ago from when Saddam was captured, but that's it."

"Can I use your satellite phone?"

Many soldiers have fairly regular access to e-mail and telephones. Those stationed in small places like these do not.

"We're just happy the mortarman ain't hit our satellite dish yet," one of them says.

Baghdad
12.25.03

Christmas is really a nonholiday here, although some guys down the street are selling trees that they cut up north. There were some grenade attacks on the Sheraton. The guerillas even managed to get the eighth floor, where the KBR people stay. Now they won't have to leave their hotel rooms to do reconstruction work.

It has been raining all week, punctuated by the occasional bombing. In response to the number of roadside bomb attacks in the farming communities south of Baghdad, the military has been routinely bombing and strafing open fields and palm groves. The sound is impressive, especially the chain gun on the A-10s, but the results are less than spectacular. A couple of days ago Rory and I went out to the site and found that they'd bombed an abandoned military base. There were some homeless families squatting there (they were all kindly asked to leave before the bombing commenced), and the sum damage was a couple of empty bunkers and one cow—a bovine Baathist.

Brigadier General Mark Kimmet categorically denies to me that the U.S. military bombs refugees, regardless of whether they've been asked to vacate the premises first.

With the new year approaching, things in Baghdad are pretty much the same as they have been. The petrol queues are kilometers long, and there's no hot water in the hotel because of the gas and electricity shortages.

Baghdad
12.29.03

Rory has a plan. Rory loves making plans. Most of them are a little bit off the wall, but they're well-meant, so I give him the benefit of the doubt. He's disgusted by everything we're hearing about prostitution. It was illegal under Saddam (although a number of brothels were run by friends of his family), but now the market is booming. We visit a police station where seven prostitutes are being held. All are destitute and tell tales of having no other option. One is seven months pregnant and has been in a cell for nearly a week. The youngest is fifteen. Some pimps have begun to specialize in call girls for contractors.

We're trying to decide how to cover this story. Rory has gone to talk to a pimp to verify the stories, and the guy quotes him prices for girls as young as fourteen. We want to talk to more prostitutes and to show the emergence of a market for young children. Pimps, however, are not to be crossed, and we figure soldiers aren't either. Anyway, Rory and I aren't sure we're capable of interviewing a fourteen-year-old who has been kidnapped into prostitution and then walking away without doing anything to help. Rory, of course, wants to carry a gun. I'm always relieved when there's no one around to lend Rory a gun.

We're joined in our deliberations by Uzma (who has been smoking hash and isn't offering too many suggestions) and David, a *voyageur de la guerre* who recently arrived from Amsterdam. David isn't really doing anything except hanging out, as far as we can tell. Isam, the Iraqi man whose apartment I am staying in, lets him stay at the apartment and I'm gone after a week, I can't take him. No one has quite managed to figure out what his purpose here is—conversations rarely go further than rote political beliefs ("Globalization and capitalism are forces of evil") and his insistence that an Iraqi Marxist revolution is inevitable. He occasionally speaks, unprompted, about his hatred for his very wealthy father.

But David's determination to tape a fourteen-year-old having sex with a soldier is too bizarre for words. He keeps coming back to it, and we eventually ask him to leave Rory's room. We later tell women's rights groups about the pimp, but we aren't sure who we can rat David out to.

All sorts of *voyageurs de la guerre* come in and out—the random American who has no bags and five dollars and is only seen once; the French or Australian tourist looking for a ride back to Amman on Christmas Day, after finding out that no one accepts traveler's checks in Baghdad. David, too, finally disappears, despite his stated intention to stay for six months beyond the end of occupation.

Baghdad
12.30.03

In the city's central morgue, near the Ministry of Health, the bodies of three men are still unidentified after a battle between American soldiers and Iraqi resistance fighters stemming from a pro-Saddam demonstration in Al-Adamiyah.

Like the demonstration started by Hamid, this one was marked by residents firing in the air and carrying grenade launchers through the streets, as the crowd swelled into the thousands.

"B'il rouh! Biddam . . ."

The crowd drew the attention of Iraqi police and American soldiers, who sealed off the neighborhood and dispersed the mob. What happened next is, as usual, in dispute—residents say that soldiers and police fired first and Iraqis shot back in self-defense; Colonel William Rabena of the First Armored Division says that his troops were attacked with grenades and RPGs before returning fire with heavy machine guns.

What we do know is that at least eleven Iraqis were killed and an unknown number wounded. The following morning American field dressings still float in pools of blood along the street. Residents say the troops fired indiscriminately at first, then homed in on anyone who tried to help the injured.

Othman Allaa Ahmed, nineteen, was killed during the fighting.

"My brother had just gone out to play billiards," says Ahmed's brother Omar. "It is hard for the youth to go play billiards now—they are afraid of being detained."

"My brother was shot in his chest and his leg," Omar says. "His friend was shot three times. My brother told his friend, 'Save yourself, I can't walk.'"

"I was in the vegetable market, pushing a cart," says sixteen-year-old Qusay Arada, who was shot in the arm and leg. "I was trying to run away from the shooting."

Al-Adamiyah has been the site of frequent resistance attacks and was one of the last neighborhoods in Baghdad where invading troops faced heavy fighting in April—the only truly urban area that has seen sustained resistance. Since that time a sort of tit-for-tat battle has emerged, pitting the pride of one neighborhood against the U.S. Army and the Iraqi police.

Al-Adamiyah is one of the oldest neighborhoods in Baghdad, close-knit and homogenous. Residents are proud of its history as a center of Iraqi revolution, religion, and culture. The neighborhood was instrumental in uprisings against the colonizing British in the 1920s and against the British-installed king in 1958. If the so-called Sunni triangle has a center, it is Al-Adamiyah. It's an endpoint for weapons coming from Ramadi and Faluja to the west. Resistance fighters from all over the country gather here to bring the fight to American troops.

Major Imad Ismail is in command of the sixty officers at the Al-Adamiyah police station, which was attacked daily by light-arms and RPG fire until the Americans left about two months ago, drawing back to a pair of bases in the neighborhood. Now the attacks only come once a week.

"What's special about this area is that all of the people are well educated. Some of them, however, are Baathists or Fedayeen Saddam. They still support their president. They want to kick the occupiers from their country," Ismail says.

U.S. military police still work closely with the police in some stations, but Ismail says he has a simple agreement with the army: "We call them if we need them. Otherwise, we work alone."

Ismail says he requested American help to quell the demonstration because he feared that his police station would be attacked. The night before he had requested American backup after a police officer was shot and killed. He's unapologetic about any noncombatant fatalities.

"I warned the unarmed people in the streets to go home," Ismail says. "Why didn't they listen? They wanted to help [the armed] people."

Armed or unarmed, Ismail says all of the men killed in the aftermath of the demonstration were members of the resistance. At least two were from Samarra, a city about an hour north of Baghdad that has also been marked by heavy fighting.

"They consider Adamiyah the center of resistance," Ismail says.

The police are often caught between the Americans and Iraqis but have continued to conduct raids in search of weapons caches in the neighborhood.

"If we get information on the resistance, we turn it over to the Americans. We're just conducting raids to find weapons—if you take a weapon from an armed man, he becomes crippled."

Before he finished his documentary Rory was a human shield. He spent time before and during the invasion in Al-Adamiyah, and as the occupation progresses his access improves. He chronicles the hostilities in Al-Adamiyah, Faluja, and elsewhere.

His footage from July shows eight men with grenade launchers walking empty streets in a loose formation, a mockery of the American foot patrols that have become so rare. It's hot: the men are shirtless but wear red kuffiyehs wrapped around their faces, leaving only their eyes uncovered. They're stalking a much larger, better-equipped prey. They may not attack this night—if the detachment they find is too heavily reinforced, they'll hold their fire. The vacant streets are a stark contrast with the daytime, when traffic is bumper-to-bumper and women wearing full black abbiyas pass shop windows filled with contemporary Western clothing, and children returning from school fill the cafés that stayed open late until the war. Now everything is shuttered and padlocked.

Four days after the street battle in Al-Adamiyah, a few hundred people hold another demonstration, demanding to know the whereabouts of family members they believe were injured or detained that night.

"My nephew is missing until now, and there is not any news from him," says a man who identifies himself only as Juman. "We have made this demonstration today to ask the Coalition troops where our brothers and where our friends are."

"When you go to the morgue to find the body of your son or the hospital to find a wounded relative, you are arrested," says Eman Ali, whose husband, Salem, was arrested after Wednesday's fighting. "I still don't know where my husband is."

In the shaheed (martyr's) cemetery behind Abu Hanifa mosque, eighteen-year-old Mohamed Abdul Jabar reads the Koran over the grave of his brother Omar, twenty-three, who was killed during a battle on June 1. Omar was either fighting or leaving the mosque after prayers when he was killed, depending on whom you ask.

"When they invaded, we in Adamiyah protected the banks, we protected the government buildings. There was no looting here," Jabar says. "They put tanks here, but we don't need the tanks. We protect ourselves."

It is at least plausible that there would have been no looting in most of Baghdad after the invasion, had not the American policy been to shoot any Iraqi with a gun. As a result of this decision, most Iraqis were too afraid to try and defend their buildings.

"Some men came to destroy the tanks. The U.S. called them terrorists, but it is just resistance. In Islam it says we must protect our country. Under international law we are allowed to protect our country. If anyone occupies, we must fight."

Jabar, an Islamic studies student, says he has not yet decided to take up arms.

"They threaten us, but the resistance will grow. The U.S. makes new enemies every day. If I fight, I will fight for my religion. Most of these troops are without religion. They are without mercy."

Flowers sit on fresh graves nearby. The cemetery, which was opened after April 9 to accommodate war dead, holds at least sixty bodies now, including some foreign fighters who came from other countries to resist the invasion. Many of them found support in the area around Abu Hanifa.

Isam, an Iraqi journalist and one of Yunis's friends, lives in the neighborhood. As we stand in the cemetery, he looks at the grave next to Omar Abdul Jabar's. It belongs to a man killed in the same battle.

"That's my friend Abdul Wahab," Isam says. "We went to primary school together. He went crazy during the Iran-Iraq war."

Isam's experiences since the beginning of the invasion are typical of the neighborhood as a whole. As a journalist who works with Rory and me, he's caught between two sides—he fears being arrested like Yunis, on the one hand, and being targeted by the resistance on the other. Working as an independent journalist is dangerous—not that having a corporate media affiliation would be any better. Journalists from Al-Jazeera are arrested more often than employees of any other agency, generally after they show their press passes. And work-

ing for Reuters didn't save Mazen Dana, who was shot near Abu
Ghraib in August. War is supposedly indiscriminate, but when
you're dealing with American troops, it doesn't pay to be Arab.

Rory's video from June 1: After a Humvee is attacked in front of
Abu Hanifa, the rest of the patrol flees the area. Witnesses to
the attack, including at least one Western journalist, say three
American soldiers were killed and one wounded. The troops
return less than an hour later with heavy armor, and the
wounded soldier fires into the air to attract their attention.
Alarmed by the shots, a soldier atop one of the Humvees opens
fire with his .50-caliber gun, pounding the buildings across
from the mosque for several minutes, despite the lack of return
fire. People scurry off the streets and dive into stores. One man
waves a white flag from the door of a tea shop. The gunner
turns his fire in the direction of the flag.

"There are many ways to be nice occupiers, but they are not,"
says one of the doctors at Namman Hospital, who claims that at
least fifteen people were wounded during fighting after the Al-
Adamiyah demonstration. "Five of the bodies were brought
here. One of the doctors saw bodies near the main square—no
one tried to take those bodies.

"I think the U.S. Army has lost their brain," the doctor said.
"They are psychologically disturbed. They shoot at anyone."

Outside the hospital, next to a flag announcing the death of
another shaheed (a label applied to anyone killed by the U.S.
Army), a yellowing flyer, purportedly from the resistance,
denies involvement in suicide bombing attacks like the one on
the Baghdad Red Cross office in October. A magazine claiming
to be published by the resistance has also appeared. It claims
that most of the resistance fighters are taking up arms to
defend their country, not the fallen government.

More video from June 1: Mohamed Qasim lies in a bed at Namman Hospital, his mother by his side. He was wounded when

troops opened fire on a row of restaurants and shops in response to an attack. There were four other men in the hospital with him, but they've all left, fleeing ahead of the troops who are sure to arrive. Mohamed is unable to leave, tethered to the colostomy bag by his side. He agrees to an interview while frightened doctors warn the cameraman to hide his equipment if the soldiers appear. The man and his mother are both terrified that the Americans will come to "finish him off."

Colonel William Rabena of the First Armored is in command of soldiers in three north Baghdad neighborhoods, including Al-Adamiyah.

"Adamiyah is not the only place we have, but it's been our most challenging," Rabena says. "It's still a combat zone.

"The people in Adamiyah consider it the centerpiece of Baghdad—I am reminded often of that," he says.

Three American soldiers have been killed in Al-Adamiyah and twenty-five wounded since May 1, but Rabena says that the resistance had trailed off.

According to his account, the army is repeatedly engaging the same core of resistance fighters. Two of the men wounded and captured after the demonstration, he says, bore gunshot wounds that he believes his troops inflicted during an attack and short battle the previous evening.

"They're more organized, but that's the nature of Adamiyah," he says.

Rabena is proud of the work his soldiers have done to quell hostilities. He ticks off a list of army-funded projects, including the reconstruction of a local orphanage, the installation of Internet connections in neighborhood schools, and repair work at Namman Hospital. Some of his offers have been refused, however, including one to help reconstruct parts of the Abu Hanifa mosque that were damaged during the April fighting. The men at the mosque have insisted on paying for that work themselves.

Rabena is convinced that things are getting better, and that the longer he and his men work in the area, the better their intelligence becomes.

"We usually go into cafés—that's where most of them are meeting," Rabena says. "One thing about having been in sector so long, we've got faces, we've got names. We don't just round them up. . . . We rarely react on something that's single-source. . . . One of the things is that these guys just can't keep their mouths shut."

Sitting in a recently raided café, a group of Iraqi men recounts the events of the week since Saddam's capture. The Americans have repeatedly sealed off the neighborhood, sometimes for ten hours at a time. And they claim that a recent spate of arrests is nothing more than a series of indiscriminate roundups. The area has been hard hit by arrests since June, when the resistance attacks began in earnest.

"When we say 'no' to the occupation we do not say 'yes' to Saddam Hussein," proclaims a man named Saif, who acts as a spokesman for the group but asks that his last name not be printed. "I was arrested by Saddam. But when Saddam was arrested, we still consider him an Iraqi.

"The arrests are to make the area weak," he goes on. His son Omar was arrested on September 28 as he left a bakery with bread for a holiday meal.

"They say he is accused of attacking Coalition forces," Saif says. "We are proud of this charge. We want the soldiers to leave.

"Omar worked at a club with children as a wrestling coach," he adds. "They said he was encouraging children to resist. Now he will train the men in Abu Ghraib."

The accounting of arrests by neighborhood residents stands in stark contrast to the information provided by Colonel Rabena. Rabena says his unit has detained only two women from the neighborhood. But a list compiled by a local resident of even the most recent arrests (December 22–24) contains the names of four women. And he is sure the list is incomplete.

Marwa Jassim Hamid, nineteen, was arrested with her

twelve-year-old sister, mother, and twenty-five-year-old sister on December 21. Her mother and her sister are still being held.

"I don't know why I was arrested. I have no contact with the resistance, but I wish now that I did. I would join them."

Baghdad
12.31.03

"They always kill more Iraqis than soldiers," sighs a soldier from the First Armored as he holds us back from the site of a Humvee overturned by a roadside bomb. Then he goes quiet for a moment.

"That was probably supposed to be me. I was supposed to be on that patrol."

The army closes a two-square-block area around the site of the explosion, near Mustansiriya University, on the north side of the city, for hours after the blast, while troops search houses, detain suspects, and remove the destroyed vehicles. The neighborhood, populated by two-story residential houses, is unremarkable save for the presence of an American base.

The Iraqi police who are leaving the scene have already warned us that American troops have smashed one journalist's camera after he ignored their order not to take pictures. So I try a different tactic, offering cigarettes to the soldier in front of the barbed wire barricade, who is keeping us from getting to the scene, and a number of anxious Iraqis from getting to their houses. One man is injured and wants to get some clothes from his house before going back to the hospital.

"Can you tell them to wait half an hour?" the soldier asks me. I try to explain, and though everyone seems to understand, they're clearly not thrilled. I shrug and apologize: I want it to be clear that although I've somehow become the liaison, there's nothing I can do.

"They just don't get it—the barbed wire means off-limits," he says. "We had a guy on the other side earlier try and drive through it. Fucked up his car pretty bad. He was hung up for fifteen minutes before we even noticed him."

The guard brushes the crowd back by brandishing his M16, which looks vaguely ridiculous—it's more than three feet long and he's not much taller. He makes offhand conversation as he tries to ignore their pleas.

"Look at all these ladies with their shoes," says the soldier, who's from Ohio, motioning at women waiting to go back to their homes. "They all got these fancy shoes now that they're allowed to show their ankles."

"Actually, they were always allowed to show their ankles," I reply. "Now it's worse. In some places people have been forcing women to cover up."

Behind the cordon soldiers are rounding up a group of about forty people.

"Those are the people who were stupid enough to be standing around and watching," the soldier says. "Now they're all going to be questioned and detained."

My colleagues angrily point to a man filming inside the cordon.

"That's probably one of our guys," the soldier says. "For future intel. There's nothing you could film here right now that you'd be allowed to show on TV, anyway."

The other journalists get frustrated and decide to try getting to the scene from the other side. I stick around and hang out with the soldier. I'm in no hurry to see any gore.

"Is CNN here yet?" he asks. "Those guys are usually the first ones here.

"Journalists," he continues. "I've had it to here. I was at the Red Cross after the explosion there—that's the worst stuff I've seen out here. And there's that girl who works for Fox News—you know the one? She's filming on the roof of the building, and I had to go up and get her. 'Can't I just get a little bit more footage?' she says, and I tell her, 'You can stand fast if you want, but this thing's going to collapse. An I-beam just fell out.'"

Eventually, the soldier radios his commander and offers to escort me to the other side of the perimeter. As we move across the cordoned area, some soldiers are sitting, exhausted, on the sidewalk. Others are still searching houses. One yells at my escort.

"Is he a reporter? What the fuck are you doing?"

"CO said it was okay," the soldier replies, and then, in a lower tone, just to me: "Those guys are the QRF—the Quick Reaction Force. They're the first ones who get here when something happens; they're the badasses. Guys like me just guard the perimeter. They're the war criminals."

At the other end of the perimeter, soldiers are holding still more Iraqis back from their homes. Some complain that they want to retrieve personal belongings before taking the lightly injured to the hospital.

"Hey! Where do you think you're going?" one of them asks a man who slips past the razor wire.

"My home," he replies.

"Can't. We're having a party," the soldier says.

Despite the seriousness of the situation, the troops engage in a bit of clowning.

"Hey man, you like to smoke pot?" one of the soldiers asks me. "You look like you like to smoke pot."

"Yeah, that's the reason I didn't join up like you guys."

"Hey, how's the economy?" asks one of the soldiers.

"It's terrible. Most of these people you're preventing from going to their homes don't have jobs," another journalist replies.

"When do the Saddams stop working?" the troop from Ohio wonders, referring to the deadline for exchanging old Iraqi currency bearing the deposed leader's picture.

"Two weeks," replies a journalist.

"That's good. I have five million dinars that I've got to exchange. I thought it was worth nothing."

"Why do you have so many dinars?"

"Got a bunch of counterfeit ones, too. You flip through the whole stack, and they've all got the same serial number."

"Yeah, we get those too. They're floating around all over town."

"Is it New Year's? I forgot," another soldier asks a journalist. "I've been going to a gas station for the last seven days to stand guard while people fill up their cars."

Still another reporter approaches, asking for the CO.

"Is that the guy from *Stars and Stripes*?" a private from South Carolina mutters. "Does he think he's getting through here? My family doesn't read that paper. Actually, they don't read any papers."

Per standard procedure, the destroyed Humvee must be cleared away before the area is reopened. One Iraqi child is dead, but the soldiers involved are all expected to recover and return to duty, according to Specialist Nicci Trent, an army spokeswoman. We're all skeptical that everyone could have survived such an enormous explosion.

Attilla, a Hungarian journalist whom I work with on occasion, is particularly frustrated with his inability to get footage, but he understands.

"Any army in the world would act the same way," he says as we walk away.

New Year's Eve is a good excuse to party, and we all need it. Paola and her housemates have decided to cook dinner, so the rest of us take responsibility for the beer, which has become considerably easier to find over the past few months. We're all expecting something to happen tonight, which is why we've decided to stay in. Many Iraqis we know aren't even celebrating. Afraid of what the new year might bring, they've decided they feel safer spending the evening at home with their families.

Hamid and I are returning with the beer around nine thirty when we hear a loud explosion. The car shakes. "Happy new year," he says, grinning nervously. We arrive at the house to find most of the others running outside to see the source of the explosion. Me, I hate explosions. I open a beer and head inside.

Uzma and a few others return an hour or two later with footage from the scene—Nabil Restaurant, one of the first eateries to reopen after the war, serving alcohol and fancy foodstuffs to the Baghdad bourgeoisie, has been partially demolished. I fondly remember going there with Kareem and his friends soon after I arrived, though you couldn't have dragged me onto Ar-Rassat Street this night. All those restaurants serving alcohol, crowds of foreigners. An obvious target.

The scene of the bombing is total confusion. Troops are trying to keep journalists back, and some of my former human-shield friends, who are in Baghdad to open a home for street kids, get into a shouting match with the soldiers. The argument is started by Uzma, who decides to blame the troops for the attack—not a particularly useful tactic, since they hardly want to be here either. A few days later I actually bump into some troops on the street who, after talking for awhile, complain about Uzma.

On this night, though, the troops have an advocate—John Burns from the *New York Times*. He lets my friends have it, complete with a string of expletives that would make any sailor proud. Part of the exchange is even caught on tape. He gives the shields hell for being shiftless activists, capping his speech with a challenge:

"I'm a reporter. What the fuck have you ever done?"

"Well, actually, we opened a home for street children."

Burns, who clearly had a tirade prepared and waiting, looks a bit deflated. Behind him, another *Times* reporter brilliantly comes to his rescue.

"Well, fuck you!"

All the other stuff, the love, the democracy, is sort of by-play.
The essential American soul is hard, isolate, stoic, and a killer.

—*D. H. Lawrence*

January 2004

Baghdad

1.8.04

It's three A.M., and Paola and I have been working late, finishing a translation of her report on the claims system. But to prove how safe this place has become, I decide to make the ten-minute walk home on my own. Rory and I have been staying out late just because we hate having to be in by eleven. The official curfew has been lifted. There's even a twenty-four-hour store just a twenty-minute walk from the hotel in Karrada.

But the curfew has become a habit. All the cabs are gone. Most nights you can get a friendly police officer to give you a ride, though. In fact, the streets are full of cops after eleven.

"Are you sure it's okay?" Paola asks.

"Yeah, the only people on the street are the police."

This is, admittedly, the first time I've tried it alone.

There was a long period of bombing and heavy fire earlier. I'm hoping that means that things will be even quieter tonight than usual. I'm right about the cops, in any case: they stop me within five minutes of leaving Paola's. They usually just run high-speed laps around the streets, but they'll stop anyone on the street. I know quite a few of them in the neighborhood.

Initially, the biggest problem is the packs of wild dogs. They trail me, inching closer and closer (no one believes me when I tell them this is just like Detroit), but fall back when a patrol car pulls up alongside.

I'm asked to explain where I'm coming from, where I'm going, and where I'm from, to produce ID, to sit through a lecture on being out so late. Finally, I'm quizzed on my ethnic origins.

"Oslak wein?" [Where are you from?]

"Amereeka." [America.]

"Oslak wein?"

"Amereeka?"

"Oslak wein?"

"Jidee wow jidatee lubnanee." [My grandparents are Lebanese.]

"Zein." [Good.]

Further scolding for being out so late. Then the question of why I'm out so late again.

"Moo moushkeela," I tell them. It's no problem. "There are police everywhere."

The officer laughs. I'm sent on my way, the dogs instantly picking up the trail.

"Imshee!" [Move it!]

Amazingly, the dogs actually back off when I say that.

Another police car stops, and we pretty much go through the same dialogue. There's a little less friendly chat and a little more scolding. Once again I'm sent on my way.

The third group of police officers I meet fully searches me and takes everything out of my wallet.

"Inta sahafee?" [Are you a journalist?]

"Eh." [Yes.]

"Inta sahafee?

"Eh."

"Inta sahafee?"

"Eh."

They're just like cops in the States. Same question, over and over.

Now I'm up against the car, and they're asking me to unpack the contents of my bag. I watch over my shoulder as the officer puts my money back in my wallet, short one hundred dollars. His partner is looking at the picture on the desktop of my computer. They're obviously taking a piss here.

They compel me to ride with them to the hotel. After all, I've paid one hundred dollars for the ride. To make all of this even more insulting, we're less than five hundred yards from the hotel. They tell me their names and what station they're from and drive off laughing—not their real names, apparently. It's dark, and there are no streetlights, and they speed off before I think to get their car number. I thought about asking them for my money back, but since they took it after I showed them my American passport and press pass, I figure they know just what they're doing. They have the guns.

I've been working on a story about the police and was getting tired of unproven tales of corruption. Apparently there are some things you just have to verify for yourself. Besides, these guys are only getting paid a little more than one hundred dollars a month. I wonder if I'd rob me in those circumstances. Knowing the situation they're in—police dying faster than American soldiers, no benefit pay, stuck between the invasion and the resistance—I can't help but feel sorry for them.

Baghdad
1.15.04

We're throwing a going-away party for Amber, an American member of a group of clowns who are performing at an apartment complex full of expats, when someone asks what has become a standard question.

"Has anyone seen Jim today?"

Jim is a British graffiti artist who excels at tagging concrete blast barriers at particularly sensitive locations, like the Baghdad Hotel. The Baghdad is heavily guarded (it has been the site of two car bombs) and is generally regarded as the CIA's Iraq headquarters. If it was true before, it's probably not anymore. I can't imagine they stayed put after the first attack.

Jim spent three days in a cage at a U.S. military prison for that one. So when it turns out that no one has seen Jim since yesterday, there can only be one conclusion. Our suspicions are confirmed when the Iraqi police show up with Thomas, a journalist who was with Jim the previous night when he decided to tag a nearby bank. The police have brought Thomas by to pick up some belongings before hauling him back to the cell he's sharing with Jim. The two are being charged with shooting a bank guard.

At first we handle the situation like reasonable adults. The police are offered beers (one of them accepts), and we ask whether Jim and Thomas had any weapons in their possession when they were arrested. They didn't, of course. But new justifications are offered for the detention. Jim (who was in the West Bank last month) had shekels in his wallet when he was arrested. Now he's suspected of being an Israeli agent. Thomas, on the other hand, is under suspicion because of his long beard. He looks like a Wahhabi, the police say. Am I the only one who thinks it unlikely that the Mossad and al Qaeda are working hand in hand? I smell cops fishing for a bribe.

The Mossad–al Qaeda story doesn't hold up for long either. Back at the station, the cops are now asserting that both Jim and Thomas are Jewish. The news of an Iraqi law against Judaism comes as something of a surprise. (There's no such thing.)

When it becomes clear that discussion won't free Jim or Thomas, the clowns resort to plan B—impromptu performance. Something has to be done to fill the uncomfortable silence that comes over the party as the first lieutenant hangs around our living room finishing his beer.

Pete, a Welsh royalist, is a pretty good juggler. He's balancing one ball on the side of his face while tossing the other two, serially switching the ball on his cheek. The cops are unimpressed. Then Jo comes out into the hall on her stilts, blowing bubbles. One of the officers pulls out his brand-new Glock (issued by the U.S. Army) and points it up at her as she towers above his head.

The police love these guns. I've been in more than one interview with an officer who suddenly pauses to look lovingly at his new gun and reflect upon how much nicer it is than the one he had before.

"My gun is a six o'clock," he informs one of our friends proudly, while holding it squarely on Jo.

He eventually puts the pistol away. Jo continues to blow bubbles.

The situation gets still further out of hand. Since the police won't release Thomas, we insist on following them back to the station. Six people pile into the back of their pickup truck. Two more carloads follow, as the cops happily lead us on a high-speed ride through the deserted Gotham of central Baghdad. Hamid is thrilled—any excuse to drive fast will do, especially one sanctioned by the law—and cranks his mix tape to full volume. Bryan Adams comes shrieking out of the speakers:

"WHATEVER I DO, I DO IT FOR YOU . . ."

I've been in this country for most of the last year and still can't account for tastes in music. Hamid sings along at the top of his lungs.

Once we reach the police station, some sort of plan does take shape. Hamid (in Arabic and unbeknownst to the rest of us) warns the police that I know an American general and will go to the base right now if our friends aren't released. One of the cops is considering dropping his badge and gun and bailing when in walks someone he's much more afraid of—a superior officer. The officer looks utterly befuddled. His men are cowering in front of a group of kids, for God's sake, and no one's stepping forward to explain why his station is overrun with foreigners (including clowns, some quite intoxicated) at one o'clock in the morning.

Eventually Hamid is allowed to inform Jim and Thomas of the "charges" against them. Jo manages to slip Jim a bottle of

Baghdad Bulletin, by Enders
ISBN 0 7453 2465 7

ERRATA

Page 1, epigraph: For *"on the looting by Iraqis and the Coalition Provisional Authority"* read *"on the looting by Iraqis and the U.S. Army"*

Page 39, line 24: For "Jason Burke, from Channel 4, has already identified the body." read "Michael Burke, an independent British filmmaker, has already identified the body."

bubbles, which he begins to blow through the bars. Someone from the crowd blurts out the essential question:

"Jim, what is the role of the artist under occupation?"

"To occupy the occupiers."

Jim and Thomas are released the next morning after a cursory court appearance. Photocopies are made of the shekels in Jim's wallet.

"They told me to just go out during the day if I want to paint," Jim says. "They even said they'd go with me."

Logistical Support Area Anaconda, Near Balad
1.21.04

After eight months embedded with the Iraqi proletariat, there's one thing I still *have* to do.

After eight months of chance run-ins, some less than pleasant, I'm still curious, still drawn by something I can't quite explain. I grew up in the Midwest. I'm twenty-three years old. These soldiers, these troops, these grunts, they're not much different from me. In fact, there's no real difference at all. Just luck, really, and the encouragement of parents, and a father who hated the military (my dad was in the motor pool until 1969 and just barely missed call-up to Vietnam). I could have ended up like any of these guys, on the trigger end of an M16, looking for a hajji to kill.

I know that not all of the Americans are walking around hoping for a chance to shoot someone, but some of our conversations freak me out. Uzma and I have just had dinner at one of the nicer restaurants in Baghdad (meaning they serve extremely overpriced French wine and you can order five courses without one of them being kebab), when we come across a checkpoint on Ar-Rassat Street, home to the busiest, most expensive shopping district in the country. A grunt named Nestor (at least that's what it says on his shirt; rarely do troops and I introduce ourselves in a very personal manner on the street—it prompts too many terrible thoughts for each about what might happen to the other), shorter than I am, starts to chat Uzma up. He does it with such honest desperation that it's almost endearing. He's twenty, and Uzma plays to him—making catty jokes, returning his glances.

I make idle chatter, share cigarettes, but let Uzma do most of the talking.

"Are you excited about going home?"

"Actually, I'm going to reenlist."

(Uncomfortable silence.)

"You want to know the reason why?"

"Well . . . yeah."

"I haven't gotten to shoot anyone yet."

More silence. As we stand there awkwardly, a car approaches the checkpoint without slowing down. Nestor steps into the middle of the road and points his M16 at the windshield. The safety is off, and out of the corner of my eye I see Uzma cringing like I am, waiting for the shot.

The car continues to come on, and Nestor jumps back out of the road, slamming the muzzle of his weapon against the car's passenger window as it draws alongside him and rolls to a stop a few yards beyond. He trots up behind it, gun trained on the head of the woman in the front passenger seat. The small child in her lap stares back up the barrel of his rifle.

"WHAT'S SO HARD, MOTHERFUCKER?!" Nestor shouts. The window is rolled down, and he looks inside the car briefly before angrily waving the driver on.

"Motherfucker's lucky as fuck there was a kid in the car."

Uzma and I start breathing again.

"Why wouldn't you just motherfucking stop?" Nestor asks, waving his rifle. "Is this not clear enough?"

Yeah, it's pretty clear. Most Iraqis know the drill by now. Some wave cheerfully at the American soldiers as they stop. Others mutter funny things in Arabic. Still others shoot the soldiers ironic looks. But almost everyone slows down long before they reach a checkpoint.

We stand with Nestor for awhile longer. Behind him, his platoon is clowning around. A few of the soldiers decide to see who
can drop into a four-point position and sight one of the oncoming cars fastest. I look down the road as the laser sight from one
of the guns hits the windshield of an oncoming car. The car
turns down a side street instead of proceeding onward.

"Man, if we were cops in the U.S., we'd go after that guy,"
one of the soldiers says.

I arrive at Camp Anaconda after being lost for a good two
hours. We stopped to ask directions from a private standing in
front of a broken-down tank that some other soldiers were desperately trying to fix, but were promptly sent on our way by the
gunner atop the Bradley.

"How do you get to LSA Anaconda?"

The soldier thinks for a minute.

"Well, first you got to turn around and then . . ."

"Get them out of here!"

"Huh?"

"Move! If you don't move I'm going to shoot you!"

The soldier trying to give directions just shrugs. I guess he
figures the gunner is serious. We stop again later to ask for
directions, this time outside a small base near Balad. A platoon
of soldiers are shopping in a small market that the locals have
set up near the base, a former Iraqi military complex. The
National Guardsman who gives us directions is a trucker from
Louisiana. He gives perfect directions that we manage to screw
up somehow.

One of our traveling companions, an activist fresh from
being arrested in Palestine by Israeli soldiers, takes issue with
the market's location in front of the base. "This is terrible," she
complains, as I witness the friendliest encounter I've ever seen
between Iraqis and soldiers. None of the soldiers have clips in
their rifles (this is extremely rare), and many are laughing and
joking with the shopkeepers. They all know each other's names.

"What's so bad about it?"

"They're selling things to them. It's imperialism."

"No, it's not. It's economics."

We eventually reach the base. Ahmed drops us off—me and Dave Martinez, an independent cameraman from San Francisco. The plan is to spend a couple of days with the unit that runs the combat hospital on the base. We've been there for a few hours when a seventy-three-year-old man is brought screaming into the emergency room. His arm is missing below the elbow. He was shot by a surveillance helicopter after supposedly pointing an AK at it.

The combat medic who found the man and rode with him in the helicopter is there. His work has saved the old man's life, but he and his team are simply incapable of questioning the circumstances.

"Strange a seventy-three-year-old man would be waving an AK at a Kiowa," one of them says.

I lived under a flight path in Zayouna. It was awful, especially when it was too hot to sleep indoors. I can understand what it means to get pissed off at a Kiowa. "Maybe he was just woken up one too many times and he went crazy," I offer. The suggestion is met with a blank stare and a shrug. Ten feet away, as the "hajji" screams in pain, the medics watch a David Spade DVD. No one's laughing.

"Make him scream," someone says behind me.

My friend Chaya is a medic. She gets very hung up on whether the people she brings to the hospital live or die, but these men don't seem to care. True, they've done their job well and saved a life. But they were past the point where they could take any blame for the outcome. I understand, but it's still ugly.

Ten minutes after the surgery, a few of the doctors crowd around a laptop watching grainy footage from an Apache's infrared camera—white on black. The footage is of a trio of guerrillas standing outside what the doctors explain is the north fence of the base. The helicopter is hovering a kilometer away from the men, so far that they can't hear it. One of them has a mortar tube, and the pilot has zeroed in on him.

The audio on the tape is of the radio communications between the pilot and the tactical operations center (TOC) on base. (Don't a ask a soldier where the "T-O-C" is. You get a blank look. You have to ask for the "tock.")

The pilots receive the go-ahead to fire, and one of the Iraqis changes suddenly from a white figure to a white cloud. The helicopter is still so far away that neither the dead man nor his colleagues heard the shots coming. It's a few more moments before the man's friends, standing about twenty feet away, realize that something has happened. Then they're both dead as well.

Some of the doctors cheer quietly or pump their fists in the air when the "bad guys" are wasted. Martinez and I swap sidelong glances, but before long we're being shown more pictures of blood and gore.

The base has its own language. I'm constantly making mental notes about how I should talk, based on little offhand comments from the doctors, especially about the other journalists.

"The guys from the *Guardian* were here this summer, talking about their 'resistance fighters,'" the head nurse, a portly woman who just wants to go back and see her cats, tells me.

"Resistance fighters" is off-limits. The preferred nomenclature is "hajji," which is casually applied to all Iraqis. "Bad guy" generally means anyone who should be on the hard end of a gun barrel. The seventy-three-year-old "hajji" whose arm was blown off has been classified as a "bad guy."

I'd like to tell them all about Iraq, what's it's really like outside the base, which most of the medical unit personnel haven't left since they arrived. The staff does offer some medical care to average Iraqis, but only in extreme cases—those in which "life, limb, or eyesight" is at stake. And once in awhile an Iraqi child will be allowed to stay at the hospital for long-term care.

I'd like to talk politics, but I'm already blacklisted from two units. They keep letting me back in, so apparently the public affairs officers from the different divisions don't talk. But I can tell what's appreciated and what isn't. Take this letter from one of the PAOs at the 82nd Airborne: "After doing a little research and reading some of your past articles and due to lack of credentialing, I don't think embedding with our units is likely."

I send her an e-mail telling her how flattered I am that she's read my work, but it's met with silence. The credential she supposedly expects me to have does not exist. Except at the 101st Airborne in Mosul, journalists haven't been issued credentials by the American military since Kuwait. And the 101st credentials are only good within the 101st.

The head nurse asks me to at least report that it's usually quiet at the hospital. I can't disagree with her. It's almost hard to tell what the people here like more, the stillness of the long nights or the nervous anticipation of imminent action. I promise her I'll report that it's quiet here 95 percent of the time. But when it gets loud, it gets loud as hell, lady.

Two hours later another casualty comes in—a U.S. soldier hit by a mortar round near Baquba. The doctors are able to save him, but they're unsure whether he'll lose his left leg. The shrapnel went straight through, possibly severing the sciatic nerve.

The wounded soldier will be sent to a military hospital in Germany, and from there back to the States. But for now he lies in a ward directly across from Iraqi prisoners.

His leg is amputated early the next morning, before he's flown to Germany.

LSA Anaconda
1.22.04

Martinez and I are having a cup of coffee—good, black, weak, American-style gas station coffee so hot that it melts the bottom of our Styrofoam cups—when we hear a muffled explosion, followed by two more. They sound as if they're coming from different directions.

"Is that ours?" one soldier asks.

"I think so."

There are a few more explosions and then a sustained burst of mortar fire, quick and regular. This time it all clearly comes from one location.

"That's outgoing. The other ones were incoming."

Being mortared is an annoyance.

The staff debates whether it's worth taking cover until one of the doctors comes in shouting.

"INCOMING! Why aren't your flak jackets on? Everyone inside!"

We're led with the reluctant medical unit into a storeroom in the center of the hospital. The base has been mortared so many times—at one point eighty-nine nights in a row—that no one bothers going to the bunkers anymore. Besides, it's cold and wet tonight, so who wants to sit on the ground under a piece of concrete that won't protect you from a direct hit anyway? If you're going to get your head blown off, it might as well happen while you're sitting indoors with a nice hot cup of coffee.

I wonder if this show is partly for us. Some people actually leave after a few minutes.

I was looking forward to being mortared. This, I figured, would be my authentic war experience. Shells exploding in the trenches—my friends seem to think life is all very Hemingway out here. I have to explain that it's not like that most of the time. Now, with the entire hospital staff crammed into a supply room, I can be pretty damn sure it's never like that.

I can't even count the number of journalists whose first question to me was, "I bet you have some exciting stories—did you see any of the real terrible stuff?" It made me ill.

Five or six shells explode. Someone says one landed across the street from the hospital, but none sound as loud as the RPGs that hit the Sheraton, which is about a ten-minute walk from my hotel, or the mortars that hit the palace across the river. Anaconda covers a sprawling thirty-two square miles, so those hits could be anywhere.

I'd rather be outside than crammed into the storeroom.

Besides, I don't even have a flak jacket. Someone has given Martinez one, and I hope he's filming. The scene is at the very least absurd. One British nurse in here has been a reservist for nearly a decade, she tells us, and when she asks where I'm from, I tell her I'm Special Forces.

"But Special Forces don't wear woollies!" she says, referring to my sweater.

I can only roll my eyes. I'm trying, I really am. She sounds like Mary Poppins, and I desperately want to leave the storeroom.

LSA Anaconda
1.23.04

A shuttle transports troops around the base. This largesse comes in recognition of the fact that Anaconda was formerly one of the largest airfields in Iraq. The Americans are slowly building it back up, and the troops that we meet on base tell us that the place has been "rented" for at least the next ten years. They also talk about other things.

"They tell us we have a mission at midnight, and then we go out at two A.M.," says one soldier on the bus, who has come to the base to sort out the fact that there's no money in his bank account back home. Many of the units posted at old Iraqi police stations or government buildings in the outlying areas come to the base to take care of essentials whenever they're allowed to. This guy is nineteen, in the Fourth Infantry Division, which covers everything from Baghdad to Tikrit, and has been stationed in one of the small villages nearby, conducting raids on a regular basis. They get hot food trucked from the base once a day and don't have Internet or phone service. He's pissed. He hates Iraq, doesn't like what's going on.

"Half the time the information is wrong," he says of the tips the unit receives.

"Be careful what you say, Specialist ——," a staff sergeant

says as she gets off the bus. Commanders in Baghdad insist that all raids are conducted on "verified, actionable intelligence." We know this isn't the case.

Specialist —— gets off the bus at the PX, which, as far as I can tell, was formerly a meeting hall for Iraqi officers. The PX is a Wal-Mart of sorts. Like everything else on the base, it's staffed by contracted (in this case largely Indian) workers—another fine KBR establishment. I go straight to the magazine rack. I'm dying for some English magazines—no one's importing recent issues into Baghdad—but find mostly *Stuff*, *Maxim*, and sports books. God forbid the troops should read the news. I snag the single copy of *Foreign Policy* (not great, but it'll do) and one of the half dozen copies of *Soldier of Fortune*, my new favorite. With stories like "How to Waste Iraqi Thugs," who can resist? Six months ago they reported that Syria had ended its occupation of eastern Lebanon.

The PX also offers all manner of brilliant "Iraqi" souvenirs—prayer rugs, kuffiyehs, T-shirts reading "Hard Rock Café Baghdad" or with a picture of a camel and a military base and a caption reading "Prisoner: Operation Iraqi Freedom." But the soldiers don't just come to the base for the PX or to solve their communications and money problems. They can also request leave for counseling. If their problems are serious enough, they can even be sent back to the States.

"Most of the reasons for immediate leave have to deal with money problems or an issue with a spouse," explains Beth Salisbury, who oversees a team monitoring combat stress. The team makes recommendations on soldiers' requests for stress-related leave.

"Most of them don't get a lot of sleep because they get mortared every night," she says.

In real life, Salisbury is an occupational therapist. But she's never dealt with this sort of occupation before.

"Most of the people just need to talk," she says. "Ninety-eight percent of them return to duty. Sometimes it's just a matter of putting them in contact with their families.

"We have prevention teams that live and breathe with the units in the dirt," she adds.

Before the young specialist gets off the bus, Martinez and I ask him whether he's had any contact with one of these units.

"You mean the guys you go see if you're a pussy and you want to go home? Nope, haven't met one of them."

Highway 1
1.25.03

I'm short on cash and can't really afford to pay for the ride back to Baghdad, so there's only one good option. It's a cold rainy morning, just after 0600 hours, as I wait in the motor pool parking lot. Martinez and I have asked to ride with the guys in charge of guarding the convoy, the self-styled "Tiger Team."

"You want to ride with Tiger Team? I don't know if Tiger Team will take you."

We sit down for the pre-convoy briefing but are swiftly removed and told to wait in the office. Fifteen minutes or so later we accompany some of the guys to breakfast. We ride out to the motor pool, where one of the team picks up a pair of flak vests for me and Martinez. The first Tiger Team Humvee pulls up, Sinatra pouring out.

"Chicago, Chicago . . . "

The 172nd California National Guard Transport Division has "up-armored" their Humvees, buying steel plates off the local market and hiring local welders to fashion doors for the trucks. They even cut out extra pieces for their flak jackets, which were issued without the thick, removable ceramic plates that can stop a round from an assault rifle. The jackets they've been issued will only stop shrapnel.

The men are proud of their ingenuity.

"You need guys who are civilians to do stuff like this," one of them says. "Look around—one of us manages a grocery store, one of us is a plumber with his own business—these guys actually know how to manage people."

"We weren't ready," says Staff Sergeant Steve Howell of the invasion. "We didn't have enough armored vehicles."

Howell, who's in charge of Tiger Team, is a former Idaho police officer, but he's unusual in one very particular respect:

"Sergeant Howell is our recruiter," says one of the soldiers, whom the other soldiers good-naturedly tease for being a gang-banger from Oakland.

"You mean like the guy at the mall?" Martinez asks, sarcastically.

"Yeah."

"Oh."

Howell volunteered to come out with the men he recruited, and it's clear that they respect him immensely for his decision.

"I want to know what happened to my one weekend a month," one of the guys says as we prepare to roll out.

The soldiers test their weapons before leaving the base, firing steadily into a berm for about half a minute. A couple of empty rounds from the .50-cal are ejected directly into the hood of one soldier's jacket.

"JEEEE-SUS!" he shouts when he finishes firing his rifle and realizes what happened. He sticks his hand behind his head and fishes out the empty casings.

"Hates California, it's cold and it's damp . . . That's why the lady is a tramp . . . "

We hit the road, and I'm riding in the back of a pickup-styled Humvee next to the .50-cal. I duck to avoid the gun as we fly down the road at fifty miles an hour into stiff, biting wind. The private on the gun gives me a look, the significance of which I can't appreciate because of his ski mask, but when I motion that I'll keep low he gives a simple thumbs-up. Familiar towns fly by as we leapfrog past the convoy and pull ahead to secure bridges. We're stuck in traffic when we hear shots.

"We're going to go over there," Howell says, motioning toward a row of houses set back from the road and the small dirt track that leads to them. "We're going to check it out, and then you're going to return fire."

All right. Camera out—check. Flak jacket buttoned—check. Door latched—check. Scared—check. The driver floors it, and we speed up the road ahead of traffic. Near the front of the convoy, two men have a truck jacked up in the inside lane and are waving their arms wildly in the air. Those weren't shots; it was the truck backfiring. But I've seen attacks on this road before. And when you're already freaked out, amped up on adrenaline, a backfiring truck sounds an awful lot like an AK.

We leave the convoy of cargo at the airport, picking up a bit of contraband from another unit before we take off.

"You sure you don't want us to drop you off at your hotel?" Howell asks.

"We'd love to show you around, but it's dangerous," I tell him.

"We'd love to invite you up for a beer, but we can't," Martinez says.

Later I joke with some of the guys at the hotel that Martinez and I almost brought soldiers back with us. They're quite relieved that we didn't. This has already been a risky endeavor. There are Iraqis who work with the Americans and the resistance.

Well, you can thank the insurgents for that.
The supply lines have been cut.

—A CPA public affairs officer, when I noted
that there was no Coke in the cafeteria

April 2004

Amman
4.17.04

I've spent the last couple months in Washington, D.C., trying to take a break from the war zone by freelancing on Capitol Hill. I told my parents I was looking for jobs stateside, but eventually I picked up a couple of freelance assignments in Iraq and got an offer to finish this book. I guess once you've been in, you never really get out.

The one thing that makes me sure I'll go back, long before I've figured out how, is watching a bunch of military families and other activists delivering a petition on the Hill in favor of censuring George W. Bush for lying about the case for war. Standing in front of one of the Senate office buildings, Sue Neiderer, a fiftyish woman from New Jersey, talks about losing her son, who was killed near Baquba by a roadside bomb. He'd been in the country two weeks, almost straight out of basic training, and was following orders to defuse the bomb, even though he had no training to do so.

The group holds a short press conference, and afterward I walk up to Sue to tell her that I was in Iraq, as well. She has managed to hold back tears until now, but suddenly they flow. She hugs me, and all I can do is hug her back. I'm holding back tears of my own.

"Tell them what it's like," she says.

The fear of going back to Baghdad is no longer there. That feeling in the pit of my stomach is gone. Back in Amman I have coffee and a whiskey with Fayyez at the Saraya and tell him about D.C. It's a relief to be out of Washington, free from the bureaucratic revolution underway there. But it's hard to ignore the Capitol's weird allure. The Hill is a little world unto itself, whether it's Condoleezza Rice's testimony in front of the Sepember 11 Commission (did anyone else notice how she neatly shifted blame for the whole Iraq venture onto Wolfowitz and Rumsfeld?) or waiting for the weapons inspectors to come out of a closed session with the Senate Foreign Relations Committee. "Hollywood for ugly people," Garrison Keillor called it. If so, it produces a higher order of farce than its sister city on the West Coast.

Since September we've left Fayyez with a few souvenirs from the *Baghdad Bulletin* days, among them our poster-sized printer and a stuffed wolf (I think it looks suspiciously like a dog) that was purportedly shot by Saddam Hussein. It came to one of our reporters through a colleague of the former ruler and now sits atop one of Fayyez's file cabinets, scowling vacantly down on our heads. A plastic Iraqi Army helmet sits nearby. Shadi picked it up somewhere (we shuddered to think about the fate of its previous owner) and nervously doffed it during the barrage of celebratory gunfire after Uday and Qusay were killed.

En Route to Baghdad
4.18.04

This is the first time I've ever gotten on a plane that I knew someone might have a serious interest in shooting down. It's about the size of an airline commuter jet, and it's about half full

of crusty-looking private security types and a few Iraqis of inde-
terminate purpose.

I don't feel much like talking after shelling out more than
six hundred dollars for the flight. There are inklings that Baghdad may be closed, after Iraqis protested the assassination of
Sheikh Yassin. Bush's expression of support for Ariel Sharon a
couple of days ago isn't likely to help things, so until further
notice I'm French.

I've come to dread the monotony of the fourteen-hour drive
more than the physical danger. However, there's a lovely little
saj oven sandwich stand at the border, staffed by a man from
Chicago who makes a great egg and cheese pita (it's the Middle
Eastern equivalent of an Egg McMuffin) and a mean cup of coffee. What's even stranger is that although the restaurant is on
the Jordanian side of the border, the border guards allow you
to wander across for a bite to eat while your driver is stuck in
line on the Iraqi side, waiting to be searched.

The flight has sort of a business-flight-of-the-damned feeling—a ship of fools, but some of the friendliest stewardesses
I've ever met. Everyone grabs a newspaper as they get on board,
and a few even make the pretense of reading them. Below us
the newsprint gives way to reality. The security contractors
(mostly South African) are making dirty jokes and looking
excited about, well . . . I'm not really sure what they're excited
about. Is it the Baghdad prostitutes? Or the thrill of arriving
somewhere where they're not welcome? I decided to fly on
Fayyez's advice. The minute I don't feel welcome in Baghdad,
I'm getting the hell out.

The plane is landing, a sharp banking dive that presumably
avoids a long approach and hence the possibility of a shoulder-
fired rocket. Baghdad sprawls below us, unevenly bisected by the
Tigris and pockmarked with palaces. It is, as it almost always is, a
clear day, and I'm sure it will be hot when I get stuck in traffic on
the way from the airport. I'm just relieved to find that my luggage
wasn't lost. It happened to a couple of the guys on the flight.

Baghdad
4.23.04

Who would turn down an invitation to a party in the Green
Zone, that former Baathist palace that now belongs squarely to
the American-led administration? They have Miller Genuine
Draft in there. God bless the PX.

Last night's shindig was a send-off for members of the
National Mine Action Center, whose mission is to find and
destroy unexploded ordnance and train locals to do the same.
So don't let the bombings in Basra get you down, or the fact
that you knew a couple of those security contractors who got
whacked the other day. The mines will soon be cleared.

The guerillas are really taking a specific interest in subcon-
tractors these days. You can't get away from stories about people taking shots at them. The NMAC guys were attacked going
after office supplies. But what's worse? A gun battle on the way
to Staples or cabin fever? One of the contractors I talk to
describes the ammo dump (a barracks on the far side of the
palace complex) where the NMAC guys live as a "prison."

But there are happier areas of the palace complex, so we
head off to the Al-Rasheed Hotel (DoD badges, please!) to get
plastered. Saddam used to host visiting dignitaries here (Don-
ald Rumsfeld, I'm looking at you), and it's now host to a disco
every Saturday, where the idea is to lose your dignity. Since
there are only two women in this place (very, very harassed
women, I might add; it's not much better in here than outside
when it comes to the number of desperate males), I'm going to
have to be drunk before I start to dance. The mahogany velvet,
the marble, the disco ball, the empty dance floor, it's all too
weird . . . so weird, indeed, that I spend most of my time talking
to Walid, who hands out the towels in the bathroom.

After we leave the disco, one of my friends from the inside
risks his life (and his job) by taking us all the way home without
a security detail. I'm far less worried about being shot than I am
about how much my pal has had to drink. Fortunately, there

aren't too many cars out at midnight in Baghdad. I'm told there are no DUI laws in the city.

Of course, the foreigners aren't the only ones who live behind walls. There are also elite Iraqis, especially the formerly-in-exile Governing Council members, who have taken up residence in houses that used to belong to Saddam's vice presidents, wives, paramours, and imaginary friends. The GC members are a breed unto themselves, sitting back and testing the political winds, building their organizations and militias (Al-Sadr didn't really do anything out of the ordinary, in this sense). Their attitude at the moment seems to be, "Well, so what if the Americans kill them all?" When you've had a price on your head for nearly three decades, watching the opposition get knocked around probably doesn't feel so bad. A lot of these guys feel like they're owed big.

Baghdad
4.24.04

It would be naive not to expect that Baghdad has changed while I've been away. Last week some friends were held by one of the mujahedeen groups in Faluja during a trip to document and evacuate civilian casualties. They were moved from house to house, and released only after their captors were convinced that they had no ties to foreign intelligence. In keeping with the unironic tradition of Iraqi hospitality, they were well fed and handled politely. One fighter even tucked my friend into bed when she became sick. Presumably the guy put his grenade launcher down first.

After their release the researchers were denounced by the Pentagon for accusing U.S. snipers of firing on civilians and ambulances, even though they had incontrovertible proof of Americans rocketing at least one Iraqi ambulance. Doctors traveling in a second ambulance behind it were forced to watch as their colleagues burned to death.

My friends who were held were interviewed by CNN today,

and the reporters told us that they wanted to be introduced to
some of the refugees who've been pouring into Baghdad from
Faluja. (The Iraqi Red Crescent estimates that two hundred
thousand of Faluja's three hundred thousand residents have
fled their city.) So we've made it all the way to the western edge
of Baghdad, myself and a couple of others in a beat-up Red
Crescent pickup driven by an unflappable man named Qassim.
The CNN crew, in an armored BMW and GMC Suburban, is
behind us. We enter the Al-Shoala neighborhood, which looks
quite a bit like the better-known Sadr (formerly Saddam) City
to the east: open sewers, tight alleys, overcrowded houses,
median strips that double as garbage dumps, and young men
pasting posters of Moqtada Al-Sadr to the walls faster than
American soldiers can tear them down. I'm praising the CNN
reporters for showing more interest in humanitarian issues
than the average talking heads when we pass the week-old
remains of an army transport truck, burned to a crisp in the
middle of Al-Shoala's main street. As we're heading off to
request permission for the interviews from one of the local
political/religious offices that has been providing food,
money, and blankets to the refugees, the intrepid CNN team
behind us suddenly decides to retreat. Dismayed, we obtain
the permission anyway, stop for some falafel and shawarma,
and continue on.

The refugees, who'd been staying in a half-constructed
building in Al-Shoala, have moved on. We find another group a
little farther off, in one of the bomb shelters in the Al-Amariya
neighborhood. Al-Amariya's bomb shelters have special meaning to Iraqis: an American bomb struck one during the 1991
war, killing hundreds of people. Upon our arrival we're
promptly invited in for tea (Iraqis serve tea no matter what the
situation) and listen to the group's sincere assurances that
they're doing okay, even though it's obvious that there isn't
enough room for all of the family members. Families across
Baghdad have borne most of the burden of absorbing them.
The neighborhood residents have been offering the use of
their showers and inviting people in for meals.

Baghdad
4.26.04

A man named "Ahmed" has just come into my friend Abu Tha-lat's living room wearing a ski mask under his designer glasses. He gives our hands a hearty shake and sits down on the couch. Ahmed is a big guy, muscular, and I can tell before he confirms it that he's ex-military. But he didn't resist the invasion. He'd been in jail under Saddam and was relieved to see him go. Two months after the invasion, however, he began carrying out attacks on the Americans. His group, which calls itself Jaish Al-Salafi (the Salafi Army), has about twenty members, including a boy as young as twelve. The twelve-year-old has become a sort of urban legend in north Baghdad. His father was shot by Ameri-can troops as he stood in his doorway during the invasion. His mother was killed when she tried to reach her husband. The boy's alleged specialty is pitching grenades through Humvee windows. I doubt that he has killed twenty-two U.S. soldiers, as Ahmed claims, but it's possible, and I don't doubt that Jaish Al-Salafi has carried out more than 250 attacks. I don't doubt that five people have joined the group in the last week.

It's hard not to laugh when Ahmed tells us that the resis-tance won't stop in Iraq, that it will move on to Palestine and then to the Vatican.

"Tell the Protestants we are coming!" he says, shaking, unaware that he's confusing his sects.

Ahmed rants a bit about "the Zionists" and explains that Iraq is the battlefield for a war between Islam and Christianity. He speaks of Saladin driving the Crusaders out of Jerusalem and predicts the same fate for the U.S. Army.

"Al-Quds!" he shouts. "Destroy the Muslims, that is the Christians' theme."

I've heard similar things from American soldiers.

David Enders: So how does Iraq compare to Afghanistan?

Soldier (who served in "Operation Enduring Freedom"): In both places it's just a bunch of goddamned dirty Muslims trying to kill you.

Ahmed is part of the religious wing of the resistance. But secular fighters, Baathists, foreigners, and tribes have formed their own resistance groups, too. If we can build a coalition, why can't they?

It helps to keep a sense of humor in the face of all this. I ran into Nasser, a former *Bulletin* writer, the other day when I went to talk to Dr. Womidh Nidhal, an emeritus professor and the former head of Baghdad University's political science department.

"The American war against the Iraqis ended last year," Womidh says. "The Iraqi war against the Americans is just beginning."

Nasser manages to laugh about his arrest a few weeks ago during an American raid on his house. This is a man with a master's degree in political science, who works for a political weekly edited by Womidh. He has soft hands and his chief complaint against Saddam is that everyone had to serve in the army. He's at least fifty pounds overweight and doesn't exactly fit the profile of a guerilla. But he was accused of having knowledge of resistance attacks and endured three days of questioning. With a self-effacing smile he admits that the hardest part of the ordeal was that his captors didn't feed him.

Nasser and Womidh reel off the list of reasons why Iraqis have lost faith in the Coalition's promises. "They propagandize that there will be civil war if they leave," Womidh says, "but they have done more to unite this country in one year than I have done in years of work." He starts to talk about Henry Kissinger and the overthrow of Salvador Allende: Kissinger's only defense, Womidh insists, was that "the Chilean people made the wrong choice." He mentions Iran-Contra, the overthrow of Mossedegh, America's support for Saddam during the 1980s. He mentions the Iraqi revolt against the British in 1922 and is still indignant about the elections that were held shortly thereafter.

"Iraq managed to hold elections eighty years ago," he insists. "That was before we built universities and sent people to get their Ph.D.'s in America, England, and France."

Despite his outrage, Womidh remains a moderate. He feels there are ways in which a U.S. presence could be beneficial, that if the CPA were willing to grant capable civil servants the proper authority, things would at least not get much worse. But he knows that the United States has a firm grip on the rudder. It's within our power to steer Iraq toward civil society or civil war. Everyone knows it. Even beggars on the street now cry "For the sake of Bush!" when they ask for money.

Baghdad Bulletin
8.4.2003

"Kebab de resistance"

By Annasir Thabit

FALUJA—This small town about 60 kilometers west of Baghdad has recently become a center of media attention, but wandering through the streets, one is reminded of why the town is well-known to Iraqis— the town's favorite meal, the Faluja kebab, is the nonpareil of Iraqi kebabs.

There are famous restaurants where one can eat this fat breakfast (simple Iraqis consider breakfast should be kebab dripping with fat). If one eats this kebab they will discover the secret of Faluja's fame.

But the kebab is not the only thing that Faluja is famous for. Recently Faluja has become the center of the most important resistance against the U.S. occupation. One of the Faluja citizens said smiling that it is the town of *kebab* and *irhab* (terrorism). By this he referred to an Arabic comic film of the same name, starring one of the most famous Egyptians actors in the Arab world, Addil Imam. But the Falujans don't consider their resistance of the U.S. occupation terrorism, but a legal resistance.

The surprise to someone unfamiliar with the town is that the resistance is not only armed. Peaceful civil resistance in Faluja has focused the attention of all Falujans that the situation must eventually take the shape of general public opinion, facing the occupation with all means.

At the center of the united national movement in Faluja is the group of Sheikh Ahmed Al-Qubeisi. Ahmed Al-Esawy and Belal Al-Ani told of their movement in Faluja in spite of the fame of Al-Qubeisi as a Religious Islamic leader.

They describe their movement as a nationalist movement and it not only contains Sunni, as it is rumored, but some Shia also. It includes Arabs and Kurds, and all other nationalities. We, they said, will welcome our brothers, the Christians, if they desire to join our movement. Our only condition is that the person who wants to belong to this movement should be Iraqi and believe in the uniting of our country and all its sects.

The aim of the movement is to collect together all the branches of Iraqis. The movement has assured frankly that the popularity of Al-Qubeisi is the indication of popular interest in their movement in Faluja and that they have been trying to gain the vote of prominent Falujans and the chiefs of the tribes. They explained that Faluja is a tribal society and the joining of these people in their movement gives it a strong push forward.

The movement assures delivery of civil services to the people of Faluja. These include cleaning campaigns, achieving clean drinking water, getting aid from humanitarian societies to distribute them to the poor people, to build hospitals and athletic clubs and to set up local newspapers etc.

As for armed resistance they claimed the resistance had started in Iraq from Faluja and continued to spread throughout all parts of Iraq. When asked about the reasons for their resistance they gave the bad abuse of the American soldiers. The aggressive deeds in their town have exploded the great anger that existed anyway because of the occupation. They insisted that Arabs never accept any kind of abuse. Out of the many examples they gave of the bad deeds, they reacted particularly to the story of the attack by American forces on the house of Sheikh Ihyab Al-Irsan, the head of the big tribe of Zobaa, humiliating him in the process.

They confessed that there were many informants in their town but as soon as the citizens discovered them they took revenge on them, as they did on the person who told the coalition about the man who allegedly shot down an American helicopter!

When asked about their own situation as an armed resistance movement and whether they supported, rejected or stood neutral they answered we support any kind of resistance, but for the time being "we don't do any armed resistance. We prefer waiting for events to unfold."

Another movement that is having a great influence on the political society of Faluja is the Islamic Party that is participating in the governing council through its secretary general Muhsin Abdul Hameed. The party representative in Faluja told us briefly about the history of his party, saying that it is considered the Iraqi branch of the famous Muslims Brotherhood of Egypt, started in the 1940s. The reason why they identify with this party is because they have been registered by this since 1960. When the Baath Party reached the power in 1968 the activity of the party was stopped but they transferred its activity to countries of Iraqi immigration such as England and U.S., Canada, Austria, Switzerland and France. Hameed is the fourth secretary after the previous secretary resigned voluntarily in admiration of Abdul Hameed's struggle within Iraq.

The party now has 125 branches. He assured that the party has a great account because the Islamic current is the strongest in Faluja society and all the parties are obliged to take an Islamic method in their action and propaganda, even the secular parties. Al-Wifak party (Ayad Allawi Group) had called for the inauguration of their branch in Faluja in celebration of their prophet Mohammad (it is a famous anniversary for all Muslims). He assured laughingly that even if the Communists inaugurate their party branch in Faluja to behave in an Islamic way!

The representative of this party was very careful concerning the talk about the resistance against the occupation. He refused to answer a question on the truth of the ex-regime's remains and about them leading the armed resistance. He asked to register as saying "we have no relationship with the armed resistance at all. We have chosen the peaceful political method and this is our only destination.

There are other groups that have their own different methods and destinations. We don't want others to deny our own methods and we don't deny others methods."

He defended the partnership of his party in the governing council saying that "our existence in this council is considered as a big victory to us and it may be a hindrance for the council if they are moving toward something the Iraqi people do not desire. We may be the tool that draws the council to the benefit and independence of Iraq. He said the party has two votes in the council because this party is originally another branch for them, with the same ideas and principles. He gave us an example about the positive role that their movement has played in the council like the subject of making the day of April 9 a national holiday. He assured that in spite of the embarrassment that they had suffered and the pressure that they had to face from the rest of the members of the council they insisted to reject this date. He assured that this date has not been decided up till now! It seemed that their representative was embarrassed and defensive of his party on this subject. After interviews with the most important political forces it seemed that popular opinion in Faluja was absolutely against the governing council.

Exploring the opinions of the ordinary people in the street brought consistent results. Merchant Abu Adil, 40, assured that media doesn't tell the truth about the numbers of American losses in Faluja and that the real numbers is double the announced number at least.

But the American forces are skilful and fast to remove the remains of their losses and their victims before the media investigate.

Abdul Maleek is a chap working with his father in his shop and also a student in an Islamic preparatory school. He said that the deaths of the armed resistance was not arranged by the Baath party nor by the Islamic movement nor by the national movement nor by the mosques groups. When we asked him about Bin Ladin he denied that laughingly. But he assured that they are the personal deeds of young people of his age that were pushed by the bad behavior of the Americans. They did these deeds as revenge for their relatives that the Americans had killed in spite of them being civilians. He added proudly that "In Baghdad, the Americans impose curfew on you at 11 P.M. until 5 A.M. but we in Faluja impose curfew on Americans from 11 P.M. to 5 A.M."

He assured that the armed resistance is still going on even at the moment of writing this report. He showed us the remains of the armed resistance inside his small town. He proved what many eyewitnesses had assured before, that the numbers of the American losses announced was wrong because he was so shocked at it. What ever he had thought about the Americans he didn't think that they might lie in this way in spite of their being a great power; for him the great never lies or cheats.

Suddenly Faluja looked like a town liberated from the occupation. There were no Americans inside at all, the citizens have never suffered from looting nor thefts nor fires like lucky Baghdad with the existence of U.S. troops.

_____

The generals say it and so do the brass:
"It's not another Nam."
I say they can blow it out their ass.
Don't fire here and don't fire there
Even though mortars are falling everywhere.

—Part of a poem delivered by a U.S. soldier
on the street in Najaf, May 13

May 2004

Faluja
5.3.04

I've decided to make my first trip out of Baghdad since returning to Iraq. While waiting at the checkpoint into the city, we met a family who had left during the fighting three weeks ago. They've agreed to allow us to follow them to their house. We were duly invited for tea, then lunch, then tea, more tea, tea, tea, tea, tea, tea, tea . . . There's a joke about Faluja: a man's house is burning, so he calls the fire department. The firefighters arrive, but he refuses to let them begin putting out the fire until they've had lunch.

These people have been away from their home for nearly four weeks, and they act as if their goal in life is to make sure that we're comfortable. I feel terrible because I've already lied to them by telling them I'm Belgian. Rana, the translator I'm with, always kicks me under the table if I hesitate when someone asks me where I'm from, but I'd be screwed without a translator, so I don't have many options. I've also noticed that changing my nationality in a cab, especially to French, seems to mean I pay considerably less than I would if I were American.

The men of this family are proud of the fact that the Americans have been forced to pull out and proclaim that the next time the United States comes, "even the women will be holding guns." The matriarch of the family smiles and winks from her corner of the sitting room. She seems to have the dozen or so kids who are running about the house in line. I'd hate to see what kind of damage she could do with a gun.

Faluja
5.6.04

We go back to Faluja eliciting surprise from the marine whom we'd met at the same checkpoint on Monday.

"You clowns again?" the marine addresses us, offering a bag of sunflower seeds.

"Actually, we left the clowns in Baghdad."

He's a nice guy from Pennsylvania who helps us get through but can't stop complaining about the lazy Iraqi soldiers who are supposed to be manning his checkpoint. For their part, the Iraqi soldiers say they plan to dismantle the checkpoint as soon as the Americans are gone. "It's hot here, and the families shouldn't have to wait in line," one of them explains.

There are also multiple points of entry into Faluja, which the marine tells us. "Just in case my officer won't let you guys through, you go about a mile around that way . . ."

Jassim, the driver Rana works with, is bumping the same Bob Marley tape he plays every time we come to Faluja. The city is in much the same condition as it was on Sunday. We see more pancaked houses (excavation has yet to begin, and the smell of rotting corpses hangs over them like a cloud); look for cluster-bomb evidence (we find the telltale patterns in one neighborhood that housed a high concentration of mujahedeen but uncover no actual munitions); and shoot the bull with some of the locals. One of the sheikhs tells us that marine snipers used his minaret to pin down a pair of neighborhoods. I'm sure digital pics of a pair of marines grinning high above a lovely aerial view of Faluja will surface soon enough.

The shaheed cemetery continues to fill. A lot of the fresh graves belong to children. We watch the burial of an old man who had just been returned to his family after he was cut down by a sniper more than three weeks ago. The rumor is that the marines are going to resume patrols on Monday. If they do, things will definitely explode again.

Baghdad
5.10.04

Some of the toughest conversations are the ones in which some-one asks me why I would ever leave the States for a place like this. But it gets even worse:

"Well, I suppose you can go back whenever you want to. What do we do? We can't leave."

I haven't figured a polite way out of this one yet. I don't sus-pect I ever will.

I have figured out how to talk my way out of most situations here, however, or at least have learned how to sit quietly with a gun pointed at my head while a translator does the talking. Yes-terday I paid a visit to the Imam Ali Shrine, which is controlled by Moqtada Al-Sadr's very jumpy Mehdi Army. Most of the fighters are poor young men from Sadr City, the north Bagh-dad slum named for Sadr's revered father, Mohamed Bakr Al-Sadr, who openly challenged Saddam Hussein and was promptly martyred for his troubles. Al-Sadr demanded the installation of an Islamic government in Iraq and often chas-tised Ayatollah Ali Al-Sistani, the ranking Shiite cleric in the country at the moment, for keeping quiet after Saddam placed him under house arrest. Naturally, Al-Sadr and his progeny are not particularly well liked by the Shiite establishment, but they have great popular support.

None of this means much to the man whose gun is pointed

at my head at present. C'mon, man. All we want to do is visit the Al-Sadr press office.

"He might be an Israeli spy!"

Safety clicks off for emphasis—an unmistakable and sickening sound. Try not to look afraid. Try not to look afraid. Could you please not point that at me? It's still early, I've not had my coffee yet. Would you like a can of cola? It's hot out here, and they're really cold. I'm happy to treat you. Please point that at the ground. Okay, thanks, that's good. No, wait, now you're pointing it at my face again. And what the hell are you worried about Israelis for? Those were definitely American tanks I saw rolling down the street a few blocks away.

In the background, a taped sermon repeats its message of anti-Israeli hatred. Posters have been appearing of Moqtada with Hizbollah's Hassan Nasrallah. Al-Sadr is apparently trying to paint himself as a freedom fighter.

Fortunately, an elder Mehdi lieutenant comes over to see what all the noise is about. We'd forgotten to bring identification that would prove we're residents of Baghdad. Of course, nothing could stop us from handing this man a card from a hotel we don't stay at (and to be honest, I'm not sure I'd want to let him know where I'm actually staying). But he wanted to see *something*. Anything. After a little more brandishing we're finally allowed to pass.

We find the men and boys of Sadr City hard at work rebuilding the Sadr office. It was destroyed by an American air assault yesterday after troops raided the building, arresting several sheikhs and killing one. This is part of the ongoing U.S. assault against Al-Sadr supporters, including the execution of two sheikhs in Hilla on May 1. It's not the first time Al-Sadr's Baghdad office has been leveled. His guys tells us that they'll rebuild it as many times as necessary.

Dahr, the freelancer from Alaska whom I've been sharing a hotel room with, visited Faluja today to see whether the Americans will really begin patrolling. So far they've only made one incursion into the city, to the mayor's house. They left without incident, and their departure was celebrated with a sort of impromptu parade, which included Iraqi soldiers and police firing their guns into the air, shoulder to shoulder with the muj.

Amman
5.12.04

I've come to Amman for an Olympic soccer qualifying game. The Iraqi team, playing Saudi Arabia for the final berth, was a long shot, but they've pulled it off, making it to the Olympics for the first time ever. For the last two weeks I've been attending their practices in Baghdad, chatting with the guys who will soon be made into poster children for "what's right" in Iraq by the Bush administration. There are tears as the players hug each other and run up to the stands, carrying the Iraqi flag, to show their appreciation for the fans who'd traveled from Baghdad to be there.

In Baghdad people are firing their guns in celebration.

"Good. They're wasting their rounds," says a U.S. private standing next to me who has been sent to Amman to videotape the game. A handful of other journalists and CPA personnel and I were able to hop a military flight from Baghdad to Amman for the game.

Does he know that if they weren't playing soccer, the young men on the team would probably be fighting the U.S. military? Many of them are from Sadr City, others from Faluja.

After the game I run into Bassem Abbas. His defensive playing was integral after Iraq went up 2–1 early in the second half. Bassem is twenty-three, my age. Just got married. He doesn't hesitate when asked if things are better now than they were before the invasion. Even after the way some of the players were tortured under Saddam, I still can't find one who's happy about the current situation. They complain that they're owed back pay (some members of the team threatened that they wouldn't travel to Jordan for the final qualifier unless they were paid), that no one will provide them with equipment. The CPA had initially told me that the team would be taking a plane to Amman for the game, but instead they've had to make a twenty-hour bus trek from Baghdad. They've received virtually no help from the Americans, who are now taking credit for their success.

"Tell the world that this game is for Iraq," Abbas says after the game. "Show them that we are Iraqis, and tell them how strong we are."

Striker Ahmed Manaji buried a cousin killed by a U.S. missile strike in April, the day before leaving for the country for a match. But these things are taken in stride.

"Even during the war we trained," says Allaa Sitar, who plays defense. "We wanted to be the first team to give sports back to Iraq."

The complaints about lack of equipment and the humiliation of seeing their country occupied are just as bitter as descriptions of the beatings and harsh training to which the team was subjected by Uday Hussein, Saddam's eldest son and Iraq's former Olympic Committee president. Uday's extravagances—fast cars; horses; parties leavened with booze, women, and the occasional murder—were well-known, as was his proclivity for less-than-friendly motivational techniques. However, these techniques were nothing like the iron maiden–style torture devices John Burns reported finding under the Olympic stadium following the invasion.

"They would let us go to bed at midnight, and then they would wake us up an hour later. Then they would let us go back to sleep and wake us up at four in the morning and start beating us. Sometimes in the winter they would fill the field with stones, and we would be forced to train barefoot. . . . There was a prison under Saddam's palace near the airport," says Abbas, who was incarcerated there twice. "The first time was because we lost a game, and the second time was because I left the hotel by myself when we were in Saudi Arabia for a game. I went to the store to buy some chocolate. It was another player that told the security officer I had left."

Abbas is not the only athlete who complains about the way things are now.

Allaa Hikmet is a nineteen-year-old runner who has been invited to compete in the games. She runs six times a week on the gravelly dirt track at the Al-Kashafa Club, a stadium and gym in Al-Adamiyah. Though she admits that women were afraid to play sports when Uday was in charge of the Iraqi Olympic Committee, she holds no love for the occupiers.

"The U.S. deserved September 11," she says.

In front of the club, a patrol of military police has spread out across a parking lot, M16s and .40-caliber machine guns at the ready. They're guarding a pair of MPs who are crossing a sewage-filled street to enter a youth club.

"We're just checking on the kids," drawls one of the MPs. "Making sure they have everything they need."

"Need" is relative in occupied Iraq. The Iraqi soccer team "needs" equipment and training. But the Iraqi Olympic Committee—now headed by Ahmed Al-Samarrai, a sixty-something former basketball player and pal of Saddam's who defected to the U.K. two decades ago—has a plan for increasing Olympic team revenue.

"We asked the Ministry of Finance for twenty-five million dollars," Al-Samarrai says during halftime of a game between two Iraqi teams. Then he wipes his brow with a Kleenex. The basketball arena, at the country's Olympic complex, lacks air conditioning. August temperatures routinely break 130 degrees.

The IOC received ten million dollars, so Al-Samarrai recently traveled to Washington to meet with companies like Motorola to talk about marketing deals.

"Iraqi society has no experience in sports marketing," Al-Samarrai says.

The morning after the game, as the other journalists and I board the plane to return to Baghdad, the CPA flaks who cover the Olympic team are working like mad. Now victorious,

they've decided there's room enough to put the team on a
C-130 heading into Baghdad, and they're hastily trying to make
sure that a contingent of troops will be at the airport to welcome the team. But the players are nowhere to be found.
They've decided to stay in Amman for a few days. They want to
go shopping.

Najaf
5.14.04

I've come back to Najaf. There are only a few restaurants open
here. We go into one of them, where the staff laments that they
only have fish available for us. Okay, we'll have the . . . fish.

In keeping with the Iraqi tendency to gastronomic under-
statement, a four-course meal of salad, watermelon, soup, and
masgoof (fried fish) is quickly laid out before us. The few other
patrons in the restaurant complain that militiamen's errant
rockets have destroyed their houses.

"The Americans are accurate when they fire," says one guy.
"The Jaish al-Mehdi [the official name of the Mehdi Army] is
not."

One man who recently quit the militia is working for an
Arab satellite station.

"I have to feed my family," he says. He's killed a few days
later while filming in Karbala.

Demonstrations against Al-Sadr are held in front of his
headquarters at the Imam Ali Shrine. The shrine is a gorgeous
building with a gold dome on the edge of Wadi Al-Salam, the
largest cemetery in the world, more than thirteen hundred
years old. The shrine sits on the western edge of the city.
Beyond it lies a scorched plain called "the Dry Sea" ("najaf" in
Arabic).

Militiamen are countering the anti-Sadr demonstration
(which some surmise was organized and paid for by angry hotel
owners) with one of their own. They parade around in an unruly
mass, chanting and waving Kalashnikovs and grenade launchers

in the air. It's precisely because of these occasional displays of devotion to Al-Sadr that the hotel owners have no business. I look around for the fellow who insisted on pointing his gun at my head the other day, but he's nowhere to be found.

Meanwhile, inside the shrine, a meeting is being held. Al-Sadr's deputies are negotiating with local leaders. They're looking for ways out of this situation. There are fistfights breaking out between the militiamen and shop owners, who are tired of the siege. I'm guessing you'd have to be pretty pissed off to get into a fistfight with a guy carrying a grenade launcher, backed up by other guys carrying still more grenade launchers.

It's clearly time to go. We race toward Kufa and the road to Baghdad, but before we reach the outer limits of Kufa the cars in front of us begin making hasty U-turns. As they peel out of our line of sight, we see a Mehdi checkpoint up ahead and a column of black smoke just beyond. You can hear the pounding of tanks in the distance. We quickly change direction and detour past Karbala, just before the fighting starts there, as well.

Baghdad Bulletin
8.4.03

"Holy Row"

By Kathleen McCaul

KUFA—It is Friday at Al-Kufa mosque. Parked buses, cars and space wagons line the approaching roads for about a mile. Those who were too late to get inside kneel on prayer mats in the middle of the road. Despite the baking midday sun, they listen, mesmerized, as the speech of Muqtada Al-Sadr, the fiery young Shia leader, comes crackling over the loudspeakers.

He speaks of the Islamic army he has called for in the name of Al-Hawza, the Shia center of religious learning in Najaf. He rejects the U.S. government's accusation that it is a terrorist organization. He condemns the raid on Al-Hawza the day before and claims the army is needed for the protection of the Islamic people.

Said Flayah, 24, traveled two and a half hours from Baghdad to be here. He is a fierce supporter of Muqtada's army and angry about the raid.

"I have come for Friday prayer, even in this hot weather, to prove to the U.S. that I support Al-Hawza and will never let anyone be our leader except Al-Hawza. I will be the first volunteer for the army. It will contain women and children also," he said.

Many of Muqtada's supporters come from Al-Thawra, the poorest district of Baghdad. Abdul Waheed Al-Sabaree, 29, an orator and Al-Hawza student, believes the army is popular because the poor are not represented in the governing council and it gives them a voice.

"The count was 1.2 million at the last stats. All the volunteers of this army are decent people, not collected off the streets. There are no intruders because each man must have a recommendation from his Imam," he said.

Thamer Raheem, 19, is a waiter in Baghdad.

"Some friends of mine joined, they told me about it. I met some guys at the mosque, gave them my name and they said that Al-Hawza will update us," he said.

Raheem's belief in Islam and the army's role in protecting his beliefs is stronger than it would first appear.

"I am an orphan and have been working since I was four years old—Islam is just like my inheritance. This army is for our sake and the sake of Islam," he said.

Al-Sadr has an ability to stir these strong emotions from his followers. After he finishes speaking, the crowd, mainly young men, immediately jump up and start racing through the streets. They carry flags with slogans such as "We will support you Muqtada" and posters of their leader. They seem whipped up, like at the end of a concert or football match. A continuous convoy of buses and cars then beat it back to Baghdad, flags streaming behind and the posters fixed to the windows.

Muqtada's might

Though his followers claim he is about 30, Muqtada's age changes with the amount of respect he commands. Al-Sabaree claims he is

34. Kassim Al-Sahlani, a spokesperson for Al-Daawa, claims he is thirty. When questioned about this he reduces his age to somewhere in the mid-20s. The men sitting in Sheikh Badr mosque thought he was only twenty.

But Muqtada has been named as the representative of Ayatollah Al-Asead Al-Haari. Al-Haari, still in exile in Iran, is a former student of Al-Sadr's father, Mohammad Sadiq Al-Sadr. Al-Haari could, if he so wished, call for jihad in Iraq through Muqtada. This is disturbing because according to one source, Al-Haari has begun to believe in Welayat Al-Fakir, the idea of a state ruled by Islamic law similar to Iran. This corresponds to Muqtada's call on July 24 for a constitution based on the Quran.

Al-Sabaree will not comment on the possibility of jihad.

"I don't think that will happen, but we cannot reject it if it does come," Raheem said.

Raheem and Sabaree both said they are willing to cooperate with Coalition forces.

"We are waiting for them to fix the security situation, after that we will ask them to leave. Only when they violate our beliefs will we start an armed struggle against them," said Al-Sabaree.

Muqtada claims his army is untrained and unarmed, simply a display of power. But members of the army laugh when questioned about their training. All Iraqis have had military training and most have guns.

Military tensions

The army has caused divisions between the Shia leaders and groups. Inad Abdulla is a regular at Al-Thawra's Sheikh Badr mosque.

"Muqtada's followers are fundamental guys, everything is exaggerated by them—we have to be united and at the moment it is not of benefit to resist the Americans," Abdullah said. "We are still waiting and we have to wait for the finishing of the governing council," he said, sitting in the courtyard of the mosque.

The Supreme Council of the Islamic Revolution in Iraq and Al-Daawa are Shia groups who now sit on the governing council. Both parties have a history of military resistance.

SCIRI's Badr troops had secret cells all over Iraq before the fall of the ex-regime. Al-Daawa's military wing, Sahid Al-Sadr (named for Muqtada's grandfather), staged what is known as the first suicide bomb attack on the Iraqi embassy in Beirut in December 1981. Attacks against both groups continued until the fall of the ex-regime. Many everyday citizens were executed simply for being members of Al-Daawa.

Despite this background, neither party supports Muqtada's army.

"It is the job of the government to form the army," said Kassim Al-Shahlani, a spokesperson for Al-Daawa.

Al-Sabaree disagrees.

"That army will serve under the ex-regime just as the previous army was working for Saddam, this army will be working without wages to serve religion," he said.

An agent for Mohammad Sadiq Al-Sadr said that he had no relations with any political parties.

The tip of the iceberg

The division that has been caused by Muqtada's army is indicative of the different approaches to politics within the Shia. Sheikh Hammam Hamoudi is political advisor to the head of the SCIRI. He draws attention to the lack of communication within Al-Hawza in his criticism of Muqtada's speech.

"I heard about this army at Friday prayers but I don't know anything about its nature or mechanism—I think such an invitation should be discussed with all members and references," he said. He wasn't sure who had decided to let Muqtada speak at Friday prayers.

Hamoudi actually has remarkably similar aims to Muqtada. He believes that SCIRI's role on the governing council is to enable the Iraqi people to rule themselves and block any reason to let the Americans stay.

But Sheikh Hassan Al-Zarghani, 33, media officer of Al-Hawza, still rejects SCIRI as "agents of the USA."

"The governing council which has been formed lately by Bremer is completely rejected by Al-Hawza. If I'm thirsty you should not bring me diseased water—I'd prefer to go thirsty. We have a complete and absolute boycott—and we transfer this attitude to a lot of people," he said.

All those sitting in the courtyard of Al-Badr mosque were sure this was wrong.

"The press officer should not express his personal attitude in the name of Al-Hawza. SCIRI is a famous front—we respect them a lot. They have been a major support for Al-Hawza," said Atabi.

A family legacy

The root of this split in the Iraqi Shia can be traced to 1999, when Muqtada's father, Mohammad Sadiq Al-Sadr, was assassinated with two of his sons. Sadiq Al-Sadr was spiritual leader of the Iraqi Shia. He was an outspoken critic of the ex-regime and favored a plan to establish an Islamic state not only in Iraq but throughout the Islamic world.

Al-Sadr was succeeded by Grand Ayatollah Sistani, now 72. Sistani is more moderate and has tried to keep religion and politics separate. He does not favor the creation of an Islamic state.

"Sistani is much loved—he has the medium way between. Within the recent situation, he said 'Don't help the ex-regime or the USA, just stay in your houses,' " Atabi said.

Sadiq Al-Sadr achieved legendary status after his death and some Shia continued to follow the philosophy of Al-Sadr instead of their new leader, Sistani. Although Muqtada is not yet qualified as a religious leader he is a living figure in which the followers of Al-Sadr can invest their more extreme beliefs.

Raheem follows Al-Sadr because he thinks he is more highly educated and believes an Islamic state would be "a wonderful thing."

Sabaree believes it is his religious duty to support an Islamic state, and consequently Muqtada's army.

"We have a lesson from our prophet Mohammad because he made an army to serve his nation—we have a prophecy that all sectors will be under one leader and they will be united with the Twelfth Imam," said Sabaree.

One agent of Muqtada said that the army's main reason for existence was to prepare to welcome the Twelfth Imam when he comes to fight with Jesus Christ.

Hamoudi does not approve of this family legacy.

"We cannot imitate a dead reference. We don't believe in inheriting positions of spiritual leadership," he said.

Sistani's seal of approval

Despite the vehemence of Muqtada's followers, the vast majority of Iraqi Shia follow Sistani. It is not clear whether Sistani approves of Muqtada's army or not.

Sabaree's brother is an agent of Sistani and he is sure of Sistani's support. Another agent of Muqtada, who did not wish to be named, claimed that Sistani was an agent for Israel. Jamil Ruthan, 33, is another regular of Sheikh Badr mosque. He puts Sistani's silence down to his attempt to keep out of politics.

"It will create a problem if he says something positive or negative. Sistani keeps quiet all the time," he said.

But Sistani has been forced into the debate. There have been numerous reports that Al-Sistani's house was surrounded and threatened a few weeks ago, some say by followers of Muqtada. One agent of Al-Sadr said they had no dealings with Sistani whatsoever.

Since then Sistani has issued a fatwa stating:

"We want a constitution which keeps our national identity which the Islamic True Religion and the noble worthies are one of their fundamental supports."

The fatwa comes with approved statements in English and Arabic such as

"The occupation authorities do not possess any kind of jurisdiction to assign the members of the constitution writing council."

These are for followers of Sistani to graffiti upon the walls providing the neighborhood agrees. It seems that even for moderate Shia, politics and religion are inextricably linked.

Sheikh Abdul Hadi, orator of Ar-Rahman mosque, explains.

"The ex-regime said all the time that religion is away from politics. They were completely mistaken. Our prophet Mohammad was the leader of the nation, politics were always part of the life of the whole Islamic community," he said.

"They cannot be separated—the Islamic religion is complete way of life," said Abdullah.

Sistani's latest fatwas against corned-beef and risqué satellite channels prove this.

Ramadi
5.17.04

A car bomb this morning in Baghdad killed the current president of the GC, Ezzedine Salim. People here cheered when they saw his burning car on TV; others honked their horns in the street. I guess it's safe to say that the people of Ramadi consider the GC a failure.

I had the opportunity to see the late Mr. Salim in action a few weeks ago, at a "town hall meeting" attended by, according to the CPA, more than 150 "regular" Iraqis. In reality there couldn't have been more than 100 people in that room, including journos and army types. I'm not sure why they bother to lie about little stuff like that. Anyway, faced with serious questions about what political right the GC actually had to make laws, Salim offered ridiculous, effluent answers. Abu Thalat, my friend and translator, responded by loudly advising the gathering that no such right existed and then storming out of the room in protest.

So what am I doing in Ramadi today? Hanging out with Abu Thalat, of course. We've decided to visit the governor here, who, despite three assassination attempts, continues to walk the fine line between outright collaboration and doing something decent for the people of Ramadi.

Basically, none of the old Baathists here ever really left their posts, because everyone was a Baathist. So things are working out fine. The level of U.S. casualties seems acceptable to both sides, and most of the people just wish the Americans would go home. One man actually tells us that he didn't mind the U.S. presence until he saw the torture photos from Abu Ghraib, which bothered him because he could no longer feel comfortable practicing his English with the troops.

After speaking with the governor we participate in a lunch meeting with all of the province's police chiefs. A few dozen kebabs later—Iraqi police tend to have the same girth as the stereotypical American cop—Abu Thalat decides to stop translating, and from there on out it becomes a meeting of the Good Ol' Boys' Club. I'm not sure exactly what's being said, but since most of these guys are obviously unreconstructed Baathists, I figure I don't really want to know.

LSA Anaconda
5.21.04

Why do I do this to myself? For some reason, people still want to know what the troops think. The troops themselves are the first to tell you that it doesn't matter what they think. Anyway, I've come back to the military base to find out.

I got lost on the way here in January, and this trip is no different, turning what should have been a forty-minute trip into a two-hour ordeal. Anaconda is a thirty-two-square-mile base, and it's awfully hard to find the main entrance in the midst of all this farmland. We've been stopped several times by American patrols. The detachment that has been sitting by the side of the road since seven A.M., guarding a weapons stockpile that's to be transported and detonated, is the jumpiest group, but also the friendliest.

"Uh, could you tell him to stop pointing that at me?"

"Oh, yeah. Sorry. You know how it is."

"You've only got one guy with you? Is he armed?"

"He shoots his mouth off pretty good."

Eventually we find a soldier who can give us directions that don't involve grid coordinates, and we're back on our way.

Getting lost isn't such a big deal. Spending time with Abu Thalat is generally enjoyable, and today's topic is the Iran-Iraq war. The theme: soldiers loot stuff in every war. Why should the Americans be any different? Of course, I'm pretty sure the Americans weren't bothering to take tea sets (which were among the booty taken from one of the towns Abu Thalat's unit took over). Cultural thing, I suppose.

Abu Thalat is fond of telling the story of how he saved Basra from being gassed by the Iraqi Army during the invasion of Iran. A gas attack had been ordered on a town on the Iranian side of the border, but the wind was blowing back toward Basra. Abu Thalat found a field engineer who predicted that the gas would kill half of Basra. He sped the engineer to a general and prevented the attack.

LSA Anaconda
5.22.04

Landing on base is a little like landing on the moon. It's always rather enjoyable trying to explain to the natives what's going on off base. But then the things you hear begin to weigh you down. Statement after statement, interview after interview. You can't argue with everyone.

"I'm sure our military does not detain people who don't deserve it."

"I think John Kerry is an isolationist."

"I don't think there should be so much media coverage of what's happening here. War is hell, and the American people don't need to know that."

I feel like I'm losing my audience, and I'm all ready to start a one-man antiwar demonstration when the siren sounds. We have incoming, which means that all of the soldiers have to sit inside a building wearing helmets and flak jackets. Me, I've chosen not to wear mine. I'm already planning to cut this embed short, I can't handle this stuff . . . I'm not allowed to go anywhere without a public affairs officer, which makes it hard to ask questions. They seem to have a nasty habit of butting in during interviews.

"Remember, you don't have to answer that question." (I never said he did.)

"Maybe we shouldn't talk about political stuff." (I've already told you I came here to talk about political stuff.)

It doesn't matter too much, in the end. Most of the soldiers are juiced enough to talk right over the PAO. But the best conversations are the brief exchanges that follow the interviews.

"What's that saying—if a soldier's not complaining . . ."

". . . he's dead." (There are still, despite the military's best efforts, quite a few live soldiers.)

Or this one:

"I was thinking, the colonel got a little carried away there, and I was thinking that some of that stuff could really get him in trouble."

"You mean like when he called Democrats 'terrorists'?"

"I was also thinking of the 'bozos in Washington' comment. We don't want to end his career."

The colonel at least had his reasons. Balad, where the base is located, is an interesting place. Some of the soldiers have been able to go out and give money and assistance to the locals (mostly poor farmers), many of whom are genuinely grateful for the help. The Iraqi contractors who provide labor for the base are grateful, as well. This certainly boosts the soldiers' morale. It's easy to forget how efficient the military can be. And when you believe in that efficiency and you believe in your mission, well—I work the colonel into a blustery rage. Goddamn longhairs asking stupid questions

"I've lived in Pakistan. Pakistan has no energy resources. You know what I see out in these villages? NO DIFFERENCE. I see MUD HUTS. I see UNPAVED ROADS. I see people drinking CRAP WATER. I see people getting diseases that they shouldn't get. This place has more oil and capabilities than Saudi Arabia. But they live in hovels. They live in huts. If I walk into a village out here, it's just like a village in Pakistan. Or Afghanistan.

There is no excuse for the infrastructure of this country to be in this state. They don't even put asphalt down. What's asphalt made out of? It's made out of oil."

The white man's burden is alive and well.

Soldiers are followers. I ask many of them whom they plan to vote for. The overwhelming answer, of course, is an emphatic "Bush!"

"Why?"

"He means what he says."

"He's a strong leader."

Funny. Those are the same reasons many Iraqis give for liking Saddam Hussein.

The mortar attacks rarely hit anything at Anaconda. The shells are usually fired from the back of a pickup truck, sometimes on the run. But the other day they did kill two Filipino KBR employees. Gina, one of their surviving countrywomen, works ten hours a day, seven days a week, for five hundred dollars a month. She's in month four of her two-year KBR contract. And she's scared. Scared of quitting and going back to the Philippines, scared of staying and fulfilling her contract. The soldiers don't think of things like this. They just think about what they see as the larger implications.

"If we do a good job, maybe democracy will take hold in the Middle East."

It's impossible to convince the majority of Iraqis that the U.S. military has done a good job. Even those who are willing to grant that the Americans may have good intentions insist that their departure is the first step to stability. If Al-Sadr is a problem, let the Iraqis deal with him. That can't happen until the Americans leave.

If the U.S. forces still want to convince people otherwise, maybe they should lay off the journos. But the PAO tries to bargain.

"We just don't want you to surprise us with what you write.

There was that article in *Rolling Stone* about the sex at West Point—no one thought that reporter was going to write that."

"What?" I think to myself. "There's no sex scandal to write about here. Is there?"

Anaconda is the driest place I've ever been. The senior officers have been telling the troops that it's improper to drink in Iraq. I've assured them that even though there are no night-clubs, Iraqis still know how to get down. I even give them a handful of dinars, just in case they get a chance to buy beer. They've never seen the local money.

Baghdad
5.25.04

One of our more cantankerous friends (he's a recovering Baathist and a touch sanctimonious) told us the other day that he's hard at work commissioning an "Iraqi Statue of Liberty."

"It will be a statue of the man in Abu Ghraib with the hood over his head and the electrodes attached to his hands," says Hawassim. "I will put it into the back of a pickup truck and drive it into Firdos Sqaure." (Firdos Square is the site of the famous—now famously rigged—photo of Saddam's statue being torn down.) The plaza is now graced by a new statue, an abstract structure whose meaning has been the subject of great conjecture and whose aesthetics have been the target of considerable disdain. "I will invite the media, and then I will drive the statue all through the town, slowly, with them following." Makes sense to me.

People's reactions to the prison-abuse scandal vary widely. My own has been constant revulsion. Every time I see another batch of pictures I either just about lose my lunch or start to cry. If I'm watching TV with Iraqi friends and those pictures flash onto the screen, the awkward silence is usually broken by a question: "How can they rape a woman in front of her father and her brother?"

At least Abu Thalat is keeping a bit of a sense of humor

about the whole thing. He reports that one of the victims he talked to commented thusly: "The Americans brought the electricity to my ass before they brought it to my house."

There's no telling where they're getting their tips from these days. The Al-Fanar Hotel, which is next to the Palestine and inside the "baby Green Zone," was raided the other day by American troops who thought they'd uncovered a group of fighters loyal to Moqtada Al-Sadr on the seventh floor. Thirty-nine kicked-in doors later, it became apparent that the raid was prompted by a French TV crew loudly editing a piece on Al-Sadr. No word on whether they were served with a noise violation.

I'm being booted from the Green Zone for attempting to interview some of the Iraqi families who live inside it. (There are about six hundred apartments and at least a few dozen houses here.) Apparently, one now needs a press escort from the military or the CPA in order to speak to the residents.

"I don't understand it either," one soldier apologizes as his partner leafs through my notebook. He chuckles a bit as he reads . . . the Iraqis didn't have much to say: it's a pain in the ass waiting at the checkpoints for hours on end; the shopkeepers inside have doubled their prices; and even though they like their new neighbors well enough, it stinks being prime targets for the insurgents.

Looks like I'll be back with the military tomorrow, so meanwhile I make a trip north to Sadr City, to check out the (newly rebuilt) Sadr office. Dozens of men are waiting here for their fighting papers after hearing about the fighting at the Saleh Mosque in Kufa. The Saleh Mosque is down the road from the Al-Kufa Mosque, where Sadr gives his weekly sermons. These would-be fighters have also been galvanized into action by the continued fighting in Sadr City. After stopping by the office, we go to the funeral of one of Monday's martyrs. Saloomi, my friend and colleague, requires that I sign a form stating that I won't hold him responsible for my untimely death at the hands of a Sadr City funeral procession. But the attendees are friendly, voicing determination rather than anger. Amir, the deceased, was twenty-four. His thirty-seven-year-old brother (who has six kids) informs us unflinchingly that he intends to take his brother's place.

"First of all we welcomed the Americans, but they did not respect that they are in an Islamic country. Then they started shooting randomly everywhere, and of course my brother wanted to defend his country and his religion. When I saw my brother lying on the ground with the RPG next to him, some of his colleagues wanted to take it away, but I said, 'No, it is mine, I will fight now.'"

And what of his children, should he meet his brother's fate?

"God will take care of them."

The way Amir died says a lot about the Mehdi Army, and why they don't seem to be inflicting many U.S. casualties even as they lose hundreds of their own fighters.

"He was waiting in the doorway of our house with his RPG, and there were tanks on the main streets on both sides of the block," his brother tells us. "There were fifteen tanks in all. His commander told him not to attack, that there were too many tanks. But he asked another man in his unit to cover him with a Kalashnikov, and he went out onto the street and fired at the Americans. He was shot twice, in the head and the neck."

Even allowing for a bit of embellishment (the number of tanks seems a little high, since fifteen would constitute the entire battalion for that side of town), it definitely doesn't even remotely hint at tactical supremacy. That's where we are. The U.S. military is fighting a turf war with a street gang. It is quickly becoming the quintessential battle of the twenty-first century: in a third world slum the military picks off people who have little understanding of their place in history, other than a deep conviction that their job is to resist.

The men at the funeral speak in a rhetorical style that's very common here, inserting our questions into their monologues and then going ahead and answering them for us.

"Why? Because we must fight. Why must we fight? Would

you accept this? If the Iraqi Army occupied your country and killed your people, what would you do? Would Americans accept this?"

They're hardened for battle. Are we? The insurgents aren't always articulate, but they're speaking the only language we all understand. They're in the streets, killing American soldiers.

They will commit the biggest mistake of their life if they don't let Iraqis control the security situation. . . . The people of Mecca know their city.

—Major Bassem Mahmoud, police spokesman

June 2004

Baghdad

6.11.04

I've come downstairs to make a grocery run this morning and found Dahr in the lobby doing yet another interview on torture. The subject is a middle-aged woman from Baquba who claims to have witnessed some of the worst abuse, including rape.

The woman has brought along her twelve-year-old kid, Taha, who in his restlessness starts letting fly with embarrassing non sequiturs, like the names of all the former mukhabarrat officers they know. Hawassim, the translator with a knack for finding us ex-Baathists to interview, is clearly happy to see me.

"Why don't you take Taha to the store with you?"

Fine. I'm in no mood to do interviews. C'mon kid, I'll buy you a candy bar and a Coke.

"And don't say you're American. He's terrified of Americans."

Hunh. I'm not sure how afraid he could possibly be of me— I'm only a couple inches taller than he is, bespectacled and looking a little befuddled because I've been working all morning. The only reason I've even emerged is because we're nearly out of water and I need a pack of cigarettes.

We walk out into the stifling heat on the quiet Friday-morning street. It takes us about five minutes to find an open shop, so I quiz Taha about his age, his school, his brothers and sisters. He answers cautiously, sizing me up, offering nothing. I think of all the troops who have told me that it's the "smiles on the faces of the children" that make them sure they're doing the right thing being here.

I try to buy him a Coke and a candy bar, but even at twelve he still insists on paying for them, and we do the usual dance. Who's treating who? No, put your money away. I'll get it. I've figured out enough Arabic to tell the shopkeeper not to take the kid's money, this one's on me. We're halfway back to the hotel when he decides to try me out.

"Do you like the American army?"

"No."

Taha launches immediately into the story of how they arrested his mother right in front of him.

"Why don't you like the American army?" he asks when he finishes the story.

"For the same reasons."

That's all I can say on the subject in Arabic. It's hard for me to elaborate, but it's essentially true.

Later, when I write about this, someone will inevitably say, "Well, you just focus on the bad stuff. What about all the good stuff the American army is doing over there?" I look back at Taha and imagine giving it my best shot:

"Well, actually, the U.S. military is here to free and bring stability to your country. What happened to your mother was a necessary but regrettable thing. And she's probably guilty of allowing Baathists to meet at your house, just like the army said (though she's apparently not enough of a security threat to be in prison anymore). You're just focusing on the negative things. And look, kid, you're going to have to learn this sooner or later, but you gotta break a few eggs to make an omelet. So stop your whining and eat that candy bar. Actually, hand it here. Your Uncle Sam wants a bite, you ungrateful little punk."

But I say none of this. My Arabic's still not that good. If anyone out there wants to explain all this to him, I'll give you his number. He's a sweet kid, quite sharp, I'm sure he'll get it.

After that I'm ready for an afternoon off, so I ask Saloomi, my colleague, to go to Khadmiya to find out about the worsening situation there. There were three attacks on the U.S. base there on Friday, after months of imposed quiet. The residents refused to let the Mehdi Army operate in the city for a long time, but they seem to have come around. Hiba—the translator I'm currently working with—and I take her children, Yousef and Hamoudi, to the park. Actually, we take them to Fun City, a would-be amusement park on the south side of the river, in the Harthea district. Sure, there are only two go-carts and one of them is a motorized wheelchair, but the kids love it.

I'm thrilled to be somewhere where violence seems so implausible. What could be safer than an amusement park? The electric train jumps the tracks shortly after Hamoudi and Yousef get off (Hamoudi just stands there looking at it, a sort of dazed-survivor expression on his face), but there are no mujahedeen hiding behind the moon bounce. The place is like something out of a Lebanese music video. They even have an inoffensive-looking middle-aged DJ there to pump out the latest jams: Amr Diab, Shereen, Khadim Sahar, even some MTV-type cuts. They love Shaggy over here for some reason.

The only drag is that Hiba's cousin is also here with his kids but refuses to acknowledge her presence because she's with a strange (read: foreign) man. Lest anyone get any ideas, Salam, Hiba's husband, knows exactly where we are.

It's hard not to laugh at the women in full abbiyas on the swingset. Call it an inherent cultural prejudice. I just can't help but find something mildly absurd about it all.

Thawra
6.24.04

Friday prayers in Sadr City are held outside a low-key mosque (many of the Sadr clerics now avoid their home mosques) on a six-lane boulevard indistinguishable from any other in Thawra. On most days there's a market here. The boulevard has been renamed "Vietnam Street" because, the militiamen say, "This is where we kill Americans."

Al-Sadr supporters (all men) are packed prayer mat–to–prayer mat on the ground. I have to walk barefoot in case I accidentally step on someone's mat, which happens often as I wind my way through the crowd. The ground scorches my feet. Men with water tanks strapped to their backs are spraying the crowd with a mist of rosewater.

There are at least ten thousand Al-Sadr supporters here. Could be as many as fifty thousand. It's hard to tell. Implicit in the sermon is an order for Al-Sadr's militia to suspend operations in Sadr City as the deadline for power transfer approaches.

After the sermon I'm invited for lunch at the house of a prominent sheikh, one of the local resistance leaders. His brother joins us. Both of them are wanted men and so cannot find legitimate jobs. Before the invasion they were members of the anti-Saddam resistance. They speak of Moqtada Al-Sadr's uncle, and of Hassan Nasrallah, the Hizbullah leader in Lebanon. They speak of prison. The sheikh was released in 2001, during the general amnesty announced by Saddam six months before the war. He escaped to northern Iraq but came back for his family (his wife had not gone with him because she was pregnant). His little girl, the reason he was arrested, smiles for pictures in a pink sundress. A toddler bounces across the room: he smiles and shouts "Baba!" when one of the men shows him footage of his father.

The living room is decorated with posters of Hussein, Al-Sadr, and Nasrallah. Behind one of the posters sits a homemade bomb, a wired artillery shell—"an American rat trap." It's to be used as soon as the Americans break the cease-fire. The Americans are allowed to drive the streets like everyone else, but the moment they fire a shot or invade a home, it's back on.

The sheikh's children smile for photos in the living room. They're wearing Western clothes: the two girls have on sundresses and hats, pink and blue, respectively. I wonder if they know what's behind the poster.

We ask a friend to give the family the equivalent of thirty dollars after we realize they've served us pretty much all of their food. This is also enough to buy a rat trap.

Baghdad
6.27.04

I'm stuck in traffic when I get a call from a Denver radio station that I do interviews for sometimes. It's about ten thirty in the morning where I am. I've decided to take the day off, figuring that the couple days leading up to the transition are going to be pretty hairy. We're all still wondering what the CPA is going to do to mark the handover (which some writers have begun referring to as the "hand-job"). They haven't really announced a ceremony of any sort, just sent out a vague press release advising us to show up at the convention center really, really early. After weeks of listening to seven A.M. mortar rounds landing in the Green Zone, I'm not really sure I want to be anywhere near the ceremony if there is one. But the CPA saves me (and 99 percent of the press corps) the trouble.

. "Have you heard that the transition has already taken place?" asks the guy from the station in Denver.

"Well, no."

"Do you think that's possible?"

"Well, sure."

"Is there anyone you can call?"

"Yeah."

"But you haven't heard anything?"

"Nope."

I ask the cab driver to head for the Green Zone. We're stranded in traffic for quite a while before we arrive.

When I finally do get into the convention center, it's quickly clear that everyone else was fooled as well. I find myself crammed in a room with people I haven't seen for months. It's rare to run into another correspondent on the beat like this, unless you're in the Green Zone or with the military. We're all a touch pissed off. The air conditioning still doesn't seem to work, and it's a virtual replay of last summer, the uncertainty, the confusion, the disorganization . . . It's truly as though nothing's changed. I know that when I walk outside the convention center the troops won't be gone. I know that when a soldier tells me I can't go somewhere I won't be able to tell him he has no jurisdiction.

No one will tell us what's going on. The military press officers say there will be a press conference in an hour, two hours, three hours, thank you for your patience. No one's really buying it, but most people are so defeated at this point they don't give a damn. They sit in the convention center, hot and sweaty, old and fat, waiting to be fed one last time. The CPA has apparently given up trying to pretend that even it takes itself seriously. The last CPA *Transition Weekly* newsletter was sent out almost a month ago.

We're expecting one last burst of hilarity, one last absurdly pompous answer. The same journalists who ridiculed the Iraqi press minister during the war have been reduced to this. Eventually we figure out that the army press guys, or Bremer's press guys, or whoever, have managed to squirrel a couple of people out of the room for a press pool, while the rest of us are waiting for something that's never going to come. I go back to watching the coverage on TV. That's about as good as it's going to get. The transition happened, and we weren't paying attention.

Iraq was awarded two bonus days of sovereignty when the "ceremony" was precipitously moved up. The whole thing took place in a bunker somewhere, and then Paul Bremer got on a plane, looking like he was near tears after a long coke binge. He would have signed anything they put in front of him. He was giving away something he most certainly didn't want, was giving away something he most certainly never possessed. Perhaps they picked the most fitting way to mark the day after all.

Postscript

Baghdad
7.1.04

For most of the week we've been waiting to hear what happened to Tarek, a crazy Canadian-born Palestinian med-student acquaintance who came out here to work in a hospital. When fighting broke out in Faluja on the morning of June 24, Tarek was on a bus from Baghdad. Soon after his arrival he was kidnapped by one of the muj groups. He passed his captivity at the front, living with the group's commander, until they felt sure he wasn't a spy. Then they pressured him to become a fighter instead of a medic. Fed up, he eventually left the front and returned to our hotel.

Faluja is under full muj control. I was there the day before the attack, and police told us we weren't safe even inside the fortified station. The military's air strikes have been hitting fighters' houses, but the muj, like any other army, are trying to control what information is released.

Tarek was forced to leave the front without his computer, but it was delivered yesterday by one of the muj, who was so afraid of being seen that he refused to bring it into the hotel. It's a truly bizarre movement, involving ex-regime criminals,

176

muj, Wahhab extremists, all probably funded by people who escaped before and right after the invasion. But most of the ground troops are regular Falujis.

Anyway, it was a week of nerve-wracking calls, with us as Tarek's only link to the outside world. They're killing five to ten collaborators a week, he says, and there's nightly fighting between the marines and the muj. Tarek is lucky to be alive. Abu Thalat (ever the fatherly sort) reprimands the young man soundly.

Baghdad
8.6.04

Back at the fighters' house in Sadr City, having lunch. Outside, Mehdi fighters are planting mines in the streets by digging up the pavement and then repaving over the bombs. They're preparing for another U.S. incursion. I realize with a start that on the way to Friday prayers we literally drove through a minefield. The passage between the two rows of bombs is wide enough for a car or a minibus, but not for a Humvee or Bradley. The minibus drivers wind through it all—another traffic obstruction in Baghdad. Nothing new.

After lunch we discuss the occupation.

"You said you were against it," one of them says to me. "What have you done to oppose it?"

I talk about the articles I've written. I talk about the things I've told people in the States, things they wouldn't know otherwise.

He takes a bomb out of the closet. It's a 160-millimeter mortar shell, connected to ten meters of wire. He hands it to me.

"Will you take this back to the States with you?"

Amman
8.13.04

Mark woke me up this morning with a frantic phone call from London.

"James has been kidnapped in Basra."

Shit. Shit. Shit. Shit. Shit. Shit. Shit. Shit. Shit. No. No. No. No. No. No.

All of the foreigners from the *Bulletin* except Mark and Kathleen (who spent time in Afghanistan and Kashmir, respectively) had come back to work in Iraq in some capacity after the magazine shut down. I left a week ago. Seb and Ralph were still there, as was James. He was the last person I stopped to see before I left.

He'd been working for the *Sunday Telegraph.* Mark had already called them. They didn't have any information. We went to work as fast as we could. An old fear had become real. Making the calls was like a reflex. It was in Basra—call the Sadr office. Almost certainly has to be Sadr guys if it's Basra. Do his parents know? Can we get hold of them? Fuck, TV is no way for them to find out this has happened.

We're no longer responsible for him. We aren't worried because our asses are on the line; we're worried because it's James. Funny James. Quiet James. James who had the balls to come out and work with us in the first place.

Reporters begin calling from the U.K.

"You know Mr. Brandon?"

"Yes."

"Was he prepared for something like this? Did he have hostile environment training?"

For what? What kind of training prepares you for twenty armed men, some dressed as police officers, dragging you out of your hotel at midnight?

I find myself once again forced to explain why any of us were there in the first place. Once, when Mark suggested to a reporter that he write a story about what we were doing at the *Bulletin,* the guy told us he'd only do it if one of us got killed.

James is out by the afternoon, freed by a decree from Moqtada Al-Sadr. I don't know if it was our calls to the Sadr office that did it, since by the end of the day everyone from the *Sunday Telegraph* to the Foreign Office to half the journalists in

Baghdad is taking credit. I suspect that as soon as Al-Sadr heard about the kidnapping, he simply decided it would look bad for his movement and did it of his own accord. Some people have even suggested that the whole thing was staged by the Sadr guys as a PR stunt, to allow their leader to appear benevolent and magnanimous. I don't really care. I'm just happy that James is safe.

Later, I look online to find out if any of the stuff I'd said about James being in Baghdad made any sense, but it didn't look like anyone had bothered to quote me (or misquote me) on anything other than the basics. That's fine.

A couple of days later I get an e-mail from Rosie, now in London and working for the Beeb, that puts it much better than I could have anyway.

> I have tried so often to explain to interviewers and editors over here—we could not help but end up in Baghdad. . . .
> To not go would have been a betrayal.